£5.95

Looking Back
at
Skipton

by Margaret Lancaster

Published by Margaret Lancaster
Far Fold Cottage, Wood End Farm, Salterforth, Via Colne, Lancashire.

Sheep Street by night. Photo by Arthur Smith.

Acknowledgements

MY THANKS are due particularly to George Throup and Barbara Mason for generous use of photographs and material. Many photographs of Skipton's past days are now available because George took the trouble to collect them, at a time when few others were interested. Grateful thanks also to the many people who have contributed their recollections and other material. These include Norman Dexter, Elsie Easterby, Gladys and Tom Yeadon, Jim Brayshay, Ben Lancaster, Ethel Wiseman, Winifred Sykes, Joan Vaulkhard, Percy Ogden, 'E.W.'. Dorothy Carthy, Agnes Cromarty, Fred and Doreen Atkinson, Arthur Brewer, Mrs Stanforth, Mrs Mansergh, Mr Wilfred Fattorini.

M.E.L.

Proceeds in aid of West Craven Churches

ISBN 0 9514012 1 1

Typeset and Printed by J.W. Lambert & Sons, Station Road, Settle, North Yorkshire.

Foreword

THIS is not an in-depth account of Skipton's past. There have been several excellent books on old Skipton, which anyone seeking detailed information is advised to consult. Rather, the aim has been to present an easily readable general description of former days in the Craven district, and for this reason dates have been kept to a minimum. It is necessary to see Skipton in the context of its past, therefore the early history of the town has been briefly outlined. The book however, concentrates on the first half of the Twentieth century—a half-century punctuated by two devastating world wars—and hopefully shows something of life in and around Skipton up to and including the Second War.

Much of the data herein can be classed as 'trivia', but since trivalities make up the greater part of daily living, it is hoped in this way to re-create something of the atmosphere of those times. Most of the information has been gleaned from talking directly to members of that generation of Skiptonians who remember pre-war and wartime days, but inevitably, hundreds of 'memories' remain untapped. Whilst every effort has been made to check the validity of the reminiscences, it has to be borne in mind that human memories are selective and that individuals remember the same events with different emphasis.

For some readers, this could be a nostalgic look back to the days of one's youth—to others, a little peep into a Skipton which is outside their experience.

M.E.L.

Contents

		Page
	Acknowledgements	5
1	Present Day Skipton	9
2	From Feudal Times	17
3	Outside the Castle Walls	25
4	Through the 18th and 19th Centuries	31
5	Canal and Railway — The Hey-Day of the Steam Train	47
6	Religious Life	53
7	The Forward March of Education	59
8	Taverns in the Town	67
9	The Great War 1914-1918	69
10	The Rural Community	75
11	Skipton's Manufacturing Industry	87
12	How the Town 'Ticked' between the Wars—Shops and Businesses	97
13	Thomas Fattorini (Skipton) Ltd	109
14	Living Conditions—Early 20th Century	113
15	The Old Order Changeth	121
16	Recreation and Entertainment—Early 20th Century	127
17	Not Cast in the Common Mould	137
18	World War II 1939-1945	141
19	Glossary of Dialect Words, once in Common Usage	148

Georgian Houses at the top of the High Street 1963 (Demolished)

I
Present Day Skipton

SEVERAL routes pass through Skipton, but to see the town at its best, is to come down the Bailey, by night, from the Harrogate Road, past the Castle gatehouse, when suddenly the wide, well-lit, tree-lined expanse of the High Street bursts into view. The ancient Parish Church stands alongside the Castle, yet being more centrally positioned, appropriately crowns the High Street, with the plain but dignified war memorial immediately in front. The High Street is no longer a street of houses and cottages, but as in many old towns, a street converted into shops, banks and offices, with only a few hostelries now remaining out of the many which graced the 'Street', as recently as between the wars.

Near the Victorian Town Hall, hardly changed at all, stands a fine double-fronted Georgian house favoured by previous doctors and solicitors. Nearby there once stood attractive Georgian cottages, which lent character and charm to the ancient town. The post-war period, however, was a time when planners in general felt the urge to sweep away the old and create the new, hence in 1960 these cottages were sacrificed for a modern clinic in spite of howls of protest from many quarters. Now, after so short a time, the clinic is redundant and a bit of old Skipton gone for ever. During this period many of Skipton's old houses and inns were lost beyond recall, yet hardly had the dust of demolition settled before it became fashionable to retain old buildings, and modern techniques have enabled builders to modernise buildings while at the same time retaining much of their original charm. Some towns, not then so forward-thinking, now have a greater legacy of old properties.

The entrance to the main car park is alongside the Town Hall, but until the internal combustion engine took precedence, this was a cattle market, paved with stone setts and having many small pens for cattle. It always went by the name of 'Jerry Croft', so called because the ground was formerly the home croft belonging to the Red Lion Inn Farm, the landlord of reputedly the oldest inn in Skipton at that time being Jeremiah Phillip. (The name 'Jerry Croft' is almost certainly a dialect version of 'Jerry's Croft' as the possessive 's' was usually omitted in dialect speech—'Tom wife' meaning 'Tom's wife' and so on). Most of the old inns in Skipton had stabling and shippons at the rear, some now converted into garages or put to other uses.

Char-a-banc Party at the 'Devonshire'

There are many banks and building society premises towards the lower end of the High Street, but in recent years Skipton has shown imagination and flair in the development of its old sites, one attractive development 'Craven Court' having all the charm and charisma of an elegant spa town. Caroline Square, at the bottom of High Street is not strictly a square at all, and was named after Queen Caroline, the unhappy consort of George IV.

Newmarket Street, to the left of Caroline Square, was one of the main roads out of Skipton—the old stage-coach road climbing steeply out of the town on its way to York over the moor. Here stands the Devonshire Hotel, built to cater for intrepid travellers, and the ample stabling behind was used by farmers at least up to the inter-war years.

At the other side of the High Street looking towards the Church stands the Middle Row which reduces the width of the Street at this point, the narrower cobbled street on its west side being Sheep Street. The Middle Row has often been a bone of contention, some citizens having advocated its demise in order to make the High Street wider and more imposing; but the Middle Row has, itself, managed to retain a certain amount of quaintness, and is the site of some historic buildings. Here, up a flight of steps is Skipton's former Town Hall, the prison cells still underneath where prisoners were one confined and branded, and the remains of the town stocks can be seen at the side of the steps. A wide archway leads from Sheep Street to Victoria Square, another attractive development, complete with tourist office, but formerly a closely built-up area of small terraced cottages where once the long row, Albert Street, had a paved walk down to Coach Street. At the top of the High Street is one of the town's oldest inns, the Black Horse, which still has an entrance to a yard with its one-time extensive stabling and outbuildings.

Skipton is characterised by many ginnels, alleys or snickets leading to small courts, usually known as 'yards'. On walking every one, there proved to be still upwards of twenty ginnels of one sort and another off or near the High Street. These were thought to have been incorporated in building plans as a protection against marauding Scots as they would have been relatively simple to defend, though there are some people who do not subscribe to this idea. Many of the buildings must have been erected long after the Scots ceased to be a threat, although it is also true that newer buildings were sometimes erected in the tradition of the old. Some people maintain that more prosperous citizens would have a bigger house up their own particular ginnel, with cottages for grooms and other workers. Then, of course, tradesmen plied their trades in premises up certain ginnels, and some yards were named after the people whose workshops were once there. Two things are certain, one, that the ginnels would provide easy access to the rear of properties, and two, that since cattle dealing was long carried on in Skipton's main thoroughfare, the

Mill Bridge, before 1923, still recognisable

narrow passages would be as useful in stopping straying animals, as in deterring the Scots.

Here are the names on the walls of most of the ginnels associated with the town centre; Birtwistle's Yard, Cook's Yard, Thanet's Yard, Providence Place, Kendall's Yard, Craven Court, Red Lion, Mount Pleasant Yard, Hardcastle's Yard, Sterling's Yard, Stockdale's Yard, Bay Horse Yard, and others not as easily identified. Between the wars, as children, we never ventured down the ginnels which were considered to be none of our business and someone might have asked what we thought we were doing there. Today some of the yards are more accessible or have been developed commercially.

Turning left at the castle near the old corn mill is Mill Bridge built 1628, where formerly a ford crossed the old road from York to Lancaster. This leads on to Grassington Road, and one 'gateway' to the scenic Yorkshire Dales. Gargrave Road joins at this point, where Raikeswood Hospital, the former work-house is situated, and where the Secondary Schools and now the Auction Mart are located. At the bottom of High Street, at Ship Corner, (named after two Ship Hotels on the same site, the second now converted into shops and offices), the traffic is diverted into two routes, one being along Keighley Road into West Yorkshire, and built up as far as Snaygill, which once out in the country, is now on the perimeter of the town. There used to be a number of small shop properties at the other side of the car park entrance on Keighley Road, which are now demolished. Travel further along, and on the right, one comes to Clifford House, premises of a firm of solicitors, but between the wars the home and surgery of Dr Norman Alex. Macleod, father of Iain MacLeod who was born there in 1913. Who would have thought that one of the two small boys (so I was told) who used to sit atop a wall outside, idly tossing small stones and dirt at passers-by, would one day become Chancellor of the Exchequer!

The other road is from Ship Corner along Swadford Street, reputedly one of the oldest and most historic streets in the whole town, but now largely bereft of whatever ancient charm it once had, being merely a functional non-descript straight thoroughfare, lined with shops. Here, many interesting old houses have either been pulled down or drastically modified, with only names to remind us of former glories. The name, Winterwell Buildings, for instance, is all that is left reminiscent of the once splendid Winterwell Hall, one time home of the Lambert family. Nestling among its taller neighbours, however, the picturesque Cock and Bottle Inn redeems the situation somewhat, if we can picture it in a more rural setting with perhaps a few free-range chickens scratching about outside. Many of the Swadford Street shops have been extended at street level but in some cases the upper floors retain something of the character of the large houses they once were.

Present day Skipton—by the Canal.

A more interesting offshoot from Swadford Street is Coach Street, which, though run-down between the wars, is becoming a desirable area now that the potential of the Canal waterway has been realised.

If Skipton is proud of being the Gateway to the Dales, it must also acknowledge being the Gateway into Lancashire along Swadford Street, which continues into Broughton Road. Indeed, much of Skipton's industrial development depended on trade from Lancashire via the canal and railway, and although the town's name is derived from the sheep which gave rise to handloom weaving, nevertheless Skipton's industry developed along the lines of nearby Lancashire towns with the manufacture of silk and cotton. (Since the Second War, these industries have largely disappeared and others have taken their place). Lancashire is far from the once-prevalent image of cloth caps and ferrets, and there are some beautiful scenic areas not fully appreciated by visitors.

Carrying on down Broughton Road, on the right, one passes Belle Vue Mills, formerly Dewhurst's, manufacturers of sewing cotton, and once one of Skipton's chief employers. The site of the old Auction Mart is on the left approaching the Railway Station, the railway line and nearby canal being once main arteries for the town's industrial life blood.

Skipton Castle in 1820.

II
From Feudal Times

SKIPTON was only a small settlement at the time of the Norman Conquest 1066, bearing the Anglo-Saxon name 'Sceap-tun' and indicating even then that it was a gathering ground for sheep pasturing on the surrounding hills and moors. In the Domesday survey, Skipton appears to have been smaller than Snaygill, or Thorlby. At that time the estates which included Skipton were in the possession of the Saxon Earl, Edwin, centred at Bolton Abbey, but, true to form, the Saxon Edwin was forced to relinquish his land to the 'Conqueror', and soon afterwards the forfeited estates were granted to a Norman, Robert de Romille, (from whom Rombald's Moor takes its name).

Robert's daughter and heiress, Cecilia, married William de Meschines, and their daughter, Adeliza (Alice) married William FitzDuncan, nephew of the Scottish King, David. He was supposed to have perpetrated extreme acts of barbarity towards the people of Craven, and to have been responsible for the sacking of many of their churches. It is said that at a later stage FitzDuncan repented to some extent of his actions, and presented to the local people a silver chalice in atonement for his misdeeds. Be this as it may, it is a fact that for hundreds of years, from the thirteenth century with declining impact until about 1650, the people of Craven had to be ever on watch against incursions of the Scots, who pillaged and burned, setting cattle loose and carrying women into captivity. The de Romille's tenure at Skipton was short-lived and in 1190, through marriage, the de Romille estates were joined to the estates of the Earl of Albemarle.

It happened that Skipton was blessed with a steep natural cliff—an ideal site for a castle which could withstand the onslaught of bows and arrows or battering rams, and early in the 12th century, the aforementioned Robert de Romille is thought to have started building Skipton Castle, and eventually the administration of the area was moved from Bolton to Skipton. For extra protection, a natural stream, the Eller Beck ran beneath the Castle's walls—the beck which can still be a formidible foe in times of flood in modern Skipton.

Later, owing to lack of heirs, the Skipton estates reverted to the Crown, and were at one time in the hands of the notorious Piers Gaveston, favourite of Edward II, but early in the 12th century stability was restored when the town's long association with the Clifford family began. Roger de Clifford was

Winter in Skipton Woods.

at that time granted lands in Craven in exchange for lands in Monmouthshire, as it was felt that here he would be in a better position to contain the ever present Scottish threat. So it came about that the Honour of Skipton was for many centuries held by the Clifford family—the Honour, loosely, being the land around, and administered by the Castle, including other manors held by various knights, who in the rigidly structured feudal set-up were subservient to the barons. One such family of feudal knights were the Tempests of Broughton, who, after a period of nine hundred years still live no more than five miles away from Bracewell where they are are first recorded, although their overlords, the Cliffords, and other names connected with Skipton's feudal past have now gone, or have severed their connection with the town. In all, fourteen members of the Clifford family held the Castle, the last five holding the title 'Earl of Cumberland'.

But the Cliffords had to pay a heavy price for their lands and position. In what was literally a 'death or glory' situation, the expectation of life of early male Cliffords was about 35 years, so many being killed in battle in France, (The Hundred Years War), in the Scottish Wars, or in baronial disputes.

During the Wars of the Roses, Thomas, Lord Clifford, in his Yorkshire castle supported the Lancastrian cause, entitling him to wear the Lancastrian red-rose emblem, rather than the white rose of York.

The family was in the forefront of all local and national events, highlighted by a Northern uprising, the Pilgrimage of Grace, in 1536. This followed the Dissolution of the Monasteries under King Henry VIII, when one of his aims was to destroy the power of Rome, Rome's influence being largely concentrated in the abbeys and monasteries. Monks and nuns were turned adrift having no means of keeping body and soul alive, and a formidable force was almost bludgeoned into action under the leadership of Robert Aske, which aimed in essence, to reinstate the monks and nuns to what was considered to be their rightful position. The king, fearful of the strength of the opposition, appeared to compromise, but once the rebels had been persuaded to disband he then went back on his word, and rounded up the ringleaders who were put to death. In other cases abbots and churchleaders were publically hanged from their church steeples as an example to those who might be tempted to follow suit. In this confrontation, however, the Cliffords of Skipton Castle remained loyal to the king and his break with Rome. It is ironical that over four hundred years later, it took a Catholic family to rescue the Castle from the enemy of the 1950s—apathy.

People moved about in the past more than is generally supposed. In 1662 for example, George Holmes, born in Skipton, became Deputy Keeper of the Records in the Tower of London.

The traumatic days of the Civil War in the mid-17th Century took their

View from Park Hill. The Castle was bombarded from Park Hill in the Civil War.

toll, and Skipton Parish Registers record many 'souldiers' who were 'slayne in skirmishes at Thornton, Settle, 'Rumley's More', Carleton and Skipton'. The castle successfully withstood a siege by Parliamentary forces for three years, and in the end when Castle forces surrendered, they did so with honour.

During Cromwell's attack, the Castle was bombarded from the top of what is now the vicinity of Castle Street. Other Streets bearing witness to the Civil War are Cromwell Street and Fairfax Street. The Castle was also bombarded from Cock Hill (up a steep hill at the end of Sackville Street, by a clump of trees) and artillery operated from Park Hill above Oates Restaurant. Recently small cannon balls were unearthed in one of these locations and it is possible that others might still be lying around.

Some years after the Civil War, when the dust had settled, Lady Anne Clifford was given permission to restore the Castle, albeit slighted, that is having had to reduce the thickness of certain walls so as to minimise any future threat. Due to her efforts, Skipton has one of the very few fully roofed English castles still in existence. She also built the Gatehouse with its sculpted message 'Desormais'—('Henceforth'). The Tudor end of the Castle was added when a niece of Henry VIII married one of the Cliffords.

Lady Anne had no male heirs, but her daughter, Lady Margaret Sackville, had married John Tufton, Second Earl of Thanet and consequently from Lady Anne's death in 1675, right until 1849, the Honour of Skipton was held by nine successive Earls of Thanet, whose principle seat was at Hothfield in Kent. Rarely, however, after Lady Anne's death, did the Earls of Thanet or the Barons Hothfield visit the town, though the Honour of Skipton was held under the Hothfield family settlements until as late as 1959.

Skipton had a small part to play in the shaping of America, when one of her sons, later Colonel Cresap (born 1694) emigrated. He, his sons and grandsons were military men, engaged in several battles with the Indians. Cresap became a landowner, and pathfinder, and agent for supplies in the Indian wars, later becoming a personal friend of George Washington. It is of interest that he bestowed the local Craven names of his birthplace upon his American lands.

It is said that Skipton's industrial development was inhibited because the Castle steadfastly refused to sell land and property, and would only grant short leases. About 1850, at last, changes began to take place, when the Castle authorities were persuaded to extend leases and overcome their reluctance to sell. Initially it was a slow process. Even between the wars, most houses in Skipton were leased from the Castle, and many farms, particularly in the Silsden Moor area, were still often referred to as 'belonging to t'Castle'. The Wades of Gill Bottom and the Wilkinsons of Snaygill are reputed to have

Number 1, High Street. Formerly Castle property

been tenants of the Castle for many generations.

After the Second World War, things were never to be the same again, for the descendants of the Cliffords through the female line decided to sever their long links with the Skipton estates. The land soon found buyers, but the Castle was considered to be something of a white elephant, the authorities fearing that if taken over, it would become a burden on the rates. It took a well-known and respected local family, the Fattorinis, (who had settled in Skipton in 1827) to rescue Skipton's heritage in the 1950's, at the same time fulfilling the prophecy that the Castle would one day once again be in the hands of the 'Old faith'. Skipton owes a debt of gratitude to this family, who have maintained the property and kept the Castle open to visitors—particularly now that there is a national resurgence of interest in local history.

Picturesque Canal Street

III
Outside the Castle Walls

IF WE have outlined, however briefly, the existence of the rich man in his castle, what of the poor man at his gate?

Over the centuries the Castle provided employment for Skipton's citizens, in the shape of military personel, craftsmen such as blacksmiths, weapon makers, grooms, cooks, scullions, land workers, even local coal miners (at Bradley) and so on, hence skilled workers in various trades became established in the town. As early as 1379 the Lay Subsidy Rolls record the occupations of hand-loom weavers, websters, smiths, glover, cobbler, fullers, (to thicken loosely woven cloth), tailors, draper, spicers and lodging house keeper. Skipton was then no more than a small village, with cottages straggling up the High Street on the approach to the Castle. Life was very primitive, yet knowing nothing else, the inhabitants survived with a sturdy stoicism so often lacking today when our world is disorientated if the electricity goes off or the television breaks down.

Think on it. Dirty, draughty hovels crawling with vermin, cold water carried by bucket from the nearest well, cooking on open fires using fuel which itself often had to be scrounged for, and a 'window cloth' to cover the aperture. At night, illumination was provided by tallow candle or rush light or firelight only, with a bed of straw in the corner of an earth floor on which to rest the aching bones. There was very little in the way of furniture, and clothes would be worn until they fell off the wearer's back. Winters must have seemed interminably long—no wonder an anonymous poet of 1250 wrote joyfully:—

'Summer is i-coming in,
Loudly sing cuckoo!
Groweth seed, and bloweth mead,
And springeth the wood new,
Sing cuckoo!'

Life was indeed hard, True, Skiptonians had the countryside on their doorstep, but in the town, streets were full of rubbish, and chamber pots or their equivalent, were emptied cheerfully from upstairs windows. Yes, these were the conditions in which most of our ancestors lived.

There was a great divide between rich and poor, but in a climate where

Inside the Chapel. Beamsley Almshouses.

Social Security was hundreds of years into the future, the only people who could alleviate the conditions of the poor were the rich landowners, and the rich man could not help the position into which he had been born any more than the pauper could help his.

Not everyone had a home, humble though it might be. In the 16th Century there were many homeless vagrants wandering about, unwelcome wherever they went, for in 1531 an act was passed whereby vagrants in Skipton were to be tied naked to the end of a cart and whipped through the Market Place until the chastisers had the satisfaction of drawing blood. A 'Bedle' was elected in the 17th Century specifically for whipping undesirables out of town. Females fared no better, and were publically flogged at the market cross, (somewhere opposite the present Otley Street) until flogging was forbidden in 1791.

Children generally were born at home, and in 1632, when one Ann Goodgion died it was recorded that she had delivered no fewer than 920 babies.

Margaret, Countess of Cumberland, mother of Lady Anne Clifford, was not unmindful of the plight of the poor, for in 1593 she started the building of Beamsley Almshouses, (which still stand) to accommodate thirteen poor widows. One of the almshouses—a fascinating building—encircles a chapel where the poor women were required to give thanks for their improved circumstances.

It is sometimes felt that the Earls of Thanet had little impact on the lives of Skiptonians, living as they did in their ivory castles and insulated from the problems of the poor, but research certainly proves otherwise in the case of Thomas, 6th Earl of Thanet, who at his death in 1729 at the ripe old age of 85 was described as 'The Good Earl'.

We are indebted to the Friends of Giggleswick Parish Records, who have compiled a comprehensive record of the good works of this man, who hid his light under a bushel, and whose benefactions were hitherto little known because he failed to perpetuate his name along with his good works, but the fact that help was at hand on such a scale, gives us some indication of the conditions at that time. Although Skipton was not of particular importance to this Earl, he was very conscious of the needs of the tenants and cottagers in this far-flung outpost. Records show that around 1690, when a 'dole' was due, the beneficiaries would attend the Parish Church, when, after evening prayers, (and in the absence of Thanet who lived in Kent), money would be distributed by ministers, church-wardens and overseers of the poor. In addition 179 prayer books and bibles were given out to his tenants, allowances made to various vicars, and he paid what looks like an enormous pension of £14 per year to William Mason, his former groom.

Approach to Skipton down the Bailey—not much different today

Perhaps some people took unfair advantage of these hand-outs, for by 1699 he was instructing his steward that future doles were to be to ex-tenants only, and that no-one else should share this charity of clothes or money unless they were very old and decrepit or had numerous children to support. He also stipulated that claimants should have lived in the town for seven years, which seems to indicate that perhaps 'scroungers' had moved in, in order to qualify. Around this time he also reminded his steward that those who benefitted one year should forego assistance the next.

It must have been difficult to allocate the money fairly, for Thanet next concentrated on supplying clothes to the needy, his steward buying the cloth in Westmorland, and having it made up into garments by a Skipton tailor, Charles Towgood. In 1701 he advised his steward not to assist idle vagabonds who would not work, for his intention was to help only those who tried to help themselves by their own labour, and who had led good lives. The steward was not to be deceived by those who were not deserving of help. Nevertheless, many coats, rugs and coverlets were distributed around this time, and the Earl was especially anxious that coats should be made up soon after Michaelmas and before the cold of winter set in. Not content with that, as the poor charity decreased, pensions increased—mainly to former tenants, although others could petition for them. His benefactions went way beyond what could be expected from the normal landowner. In addition the noble Earl supported a Charity school for girls, and made donations to local servants, tenants, hospitals and schools.

Further, in 1685, besides his contributions of money to the poor of Skipton Parish, he assisted hundreds of poor families in the surrounding Craven villages.

There were others, of course, who did their best to set Skipton on its feet in the 17th and 18th centuries, such as John Craven who in 1647 left £200 to Skipton's poor, with additional money for the benefit of poor scholars of the Free Grammar School. The fact that these bequests were made, enabled some poor scholars eventually to join the ranks of the middle class, when they or their descendants in turn would become employers and benefactors.

Miss Herron at work on a hand-loom (Handloom weaving was then an almost dead industry).

IV
Through the 18th and 19th Centuries

AS THE 18th Century progressed, so social conditions began to change, albeit slowly. The stocks in the market place were still being used in the 1730s, but were not taken down until the next century, the pillory being removed about 1770. During this period, 'riding the stang' was a common remedy for wife-beating, when townspeople took the law into their own hands, sang doggerel verses outside the accused's home, and generally caused a commotion to draw attention to the husband's misdeeds. Women of lewd or unruly behaviour suffered the indignity of Skipton's ducking stool, when being immersed three times in cold water was supposed to bring them to their senses.

In the early 18th century women guilty of sexual indiscretions were sometimes required to do penance in Church, bare-footed and clothed in a white sheet in sight of all during serivce—but there was no such punishment for the indiscretions of the noble earls!

Living conditions for cottagers were still primitive. Water continued to be carried by the bucket, and there were many complaints about the beck being polluted. The contents of slop buckets were still being thrown into the streets, while dung and rubbish piled up outside house doors. Butchers killed cattle themselves in numerous little slaughterhouses which were dotted about the town, and blood and offal spilled over into the streets, which combined with excrement from sheep and pigs roaming about, could not have made Skipton a very salubrious place in which to live. Further, mad dogs still roamed the streets, accompanied by the ever present threat of rabies. The perennial complaints concerning Skipton's stallholders were simmering even then, when stalls were said to be left out all night, blocking access and causing a nuisance.

The populace sought relaxation in cruel sports, and right up to 1757 records refer to the splicing and repairing of ropes used for bull-baiting in 'ye bull ring.'

Many workers were engaged in hand-loom weaving in their own homes, using 'home-grown' wool, but as time went on associated occupational offshoots made their appearance in the Parish registers, mentioning now the trades of worsted weavers, shalloon weavers (twilled worsted), stocking weavers, 'linnen' weavers, flaxmen, hatters, dyers, breeches-makers, mercers

Aireville Hall, now a Secondary School, built by Henry Alcock and later home of the Dewhurst family.

and silkmen. Others were engaged in the business of wool-combing, (one of the last operations to be mechanised). In time, industry moved from cottage homes to centres of industry run by water power, particularly after 1773 when raw materials could be transported by canal. In 1785 High Mills near the Castle Woods was built for Messrs Garforth, Blackburn and Sedgewick.

By 1822 several manufacturing concerns were already operational, including:— Isaac Dewhurst, spinner, Newmarket Street; Storey Watkinson, Newmarket Street; William Sidgewick, spinner, Market Place; James Wilson, Millfields, worsted spinner; William Beesley, Spencers Street; Thomas Hanson, linen manufacturer; James Smith, woolcomb maker, School Street; John Tillotson, Belmont; J. and W. Berbeck and Co., Commercial Street.

About this time, Mr John Dewhurst, founder of Belle Vue Mills, began manufacturing in Skipton, and around 1829 first introduced power looms, but Dr Rowley records that such was the strength of feeling against mechanisation that the machinery had to be securely boxed up, and moved into position with great secrecy.

In 1835, another industry surfaced, when the Craven Lead works was established in Keighley Road by John Fell and Foster Horner.

By the middle of the 18th century, however, it seemed that Skipton was trapped in a vice, unable to expand because of the reluctance of the Castle to sell land for development, but with hindsight, perhaps we can be thankful that this market town did not develop along the lines of Leeds or Bradford.

Dr Whitaker, whose valuable 'History of Craven' is a 'must' on every local historian's shelf, lived during these decades (1759-1821), but during this era not much help or encouragement for the workers came from the pens of the wealthy and educated. Though a clergyman, Dr Whitaker was basically concerned only with the annals of those, who like himself, could claim descent from noble families. The rest he lumped together as of little account, and it is said that he referred to 'ordinary' people as 'the other riff-raff in the churchyard'.

Similarly, Henry Alcock, born 1791, highlights the tremendous differences between the few rich and the many poor. Alcock was a prosperous solicitor, whose family had been in the business since 1732, when one, John Alcock is known to have been articled to the Earl of Thanet's steward at Skipton Castle. (The avenue to the professions in those days was still via the Castle). Henry himself first learned to read in the Sunday School or Dame School in Spencer's Yard, and as time went on, he grew to be a man of some consequence in the town. His name appears on many documents of the period, and he was, among other activities, partner in the Craven Bank. In the mid 18th century, he presided over the first soirée of the Mechanics Institute, and it is interesting to note that in spite of being the first chairman of the Skipton

The Craven Herald Office 1898.

Local Board of Health in 1858, he led opposition to the establishment of a sewerage scheme when it was first proposed. While the poorest inhabitants were existing on under 10d per week, Dr Rowley records that Alcock kept a sedan chair, generally used to take his two daughters to private school, and carried by two footmen with powdered hair, dressed in plush knickerbockers, canary-coloured waistcoats and swallow-tailed coats. Henry Alcock lived at No. 3, High Street, the imposing double bay-windowed house, lately occupied by Messrs Walker, Charlesworth and Foster, solicitors. When Henry Alcock lived there, the house was Castle property, but in 1856 Alcock built the prestigious Aireville Hall up Gargrave Road. (Now extended to form Aireville school).

We must not be too hard in our condemnation of Dr Whitaker and of Henry Alcock and his fine daughters, who lived in such opulence amidst general poverty, for their way of life was in keeping with the thinking of the age.

During the 18th Century, most children were illiterate, and education was a very hit-and-miss affair, sometimes with more miss than hit. What steps there were taken to improve the situation depended largely on the social conscience of the landowners, but later other organisations such as Dame Schools, Sunday Schools, and denominational schools played an important part. It is known that in 1715, the Earl of Burlington gave £5 for the teaching of writing to boys for six weeks in summer, and that the Earl of Thanet supported a charity school for girls in 1729. Here and there, too, a few private schools flourished. The one shining and steady light was the Boys' Grammar School, initially founded in 1492 (the year that Columbus sailed to America!) by landowner and Dean of Craven, Peter Toller, and refounded in 1548 by William Ermysted, from whom it takes its name. Many poor boys had the opportunity of being educated through the Grammar School, and gradually education facilities for the masses were extended.

As early as 1814 the first National School appeared up Rectory Lane, followed in time by Skipton's other schools, most of which were built between the dates 1837 and 1911, speeded up by the passing of the Education Act in 1870, making education compulsory for all. St Monica's Convent had been established up Gargrave Road in 1861, but the Girls' High School was later, starting life in Temperance Rooms on Sackville Street in 1886 and moving higher up Gargrave Road as the Girls' endowed School in 1889. A little before this, in 1876, Ermysted's had also moved up Gargrave Road, and so with the later addition of Aireville, Gargrave Road became the mecca for secondary education in the town.

It was a hopeful sign of increased literacy, when in 1852, the first periodical, the Skipton Advertiser and Monthly Recorder was published, followed in 1860 by the Pioneer, the Craven Herald publishing its first number in 1874.

Last days of the old Auction Mart, Broughton Road, 1989.

The spiritual development of the town took place alongside the extension of educational facilities. The Parish Church had graced the High Street since the 14th Century, and is of great historical interest, while the Friends' Meeting House was erected down the Ginnel in 1693, built partly, it is said by reconstruction of a Quaker building from Bradley, once a Quaker stronghold. Churches of many other denominations, Roman Catholic, Wesleyan, Primtive, Congregational, Salvation Army, continued to have premises built, mostly during the late 19th century.

The feudal overlords of Skipton had not been all 'take' and no 'give', as for many centuries the populace had looked to the Castle for security and protections. This being no longer necessary, the townspeople had long been throwing off the feudal stranglehold, and opportunities increasingly appeared outside the Castle walls for those prepared to grasp them. In 1833 Dr Dodgson erected the first Public Baths and Pleasure Grounds up Short Bank Road, with access to the sulphur spring nearby. Small tradesmen and businessmen more and more made their mark, the Co-operative movement was established, and public services gained a foothold.

In an obituary of 1901 in the Craven Household Almanac, we read of one John Throup (1837-1899) whose activities illustrate the opportunities ready to be grasped by an entrepreneur of this period. Originally a Rylstone farmer, John moved to Skipton, where he became landlord of the Black Horse Hotel, a not altogether happy appointment, for in his over-enthusiasm for change, he is blamed for the installation of bay windows, and the despoilation of an historic doorway. Later, John Throup took over the Midland Hotel, and realising the potential, he opened Refreshment Rooms at the Railway Station opposite. He was an auctioneer, who in partnership, established the Throup and Davis Auction Mart down Broughton Road in 1886, which operated for over a hundred years on this site, until as recently as 1990. Besides all this, Throup managed to run a thriving timber business on a prime site opposite the station, (later owned by Mr Alfred Green and still occupied by a large joinery works). Not content with that, he was also agent for the Rylstone property of Revd Canon Chamberlain, and he held an appointment under the Board of Agriculture, involving the distribution of seeds. He was a keen churchman and churchwarden, and his public duties included membership of the Burial Board, and the old Local Board which preceded the Skipton Urban District Council. He was interested in education, and sat on the Sylvestor Petyt Trust, being also an Overseer of the Poor. He was a member of the Joint Infectious Committee, prime mover in the provision of public slaughterhouses, and of the purchase of Skipton Gas Works, and he lent his support ot the Yorkshire Dales Railway. On two occasions he was Grand Master of the Freemasons, the Craven Lodge having been established in 1860. The fact that John Throup

Queen's Court, birthplace of Thomas Spencer of Marks and Spencer.
A typical narrow, dark court.
Only the name plate is left, now in the Craven Museum.

had a finger in so many pies shows how varied were the activities taking place during this period. Meanwhile, in a general sense, telephone links were being established, fire brigades improved, golf links opened and foundations generally laid for all the essentials of the next century.

Of more specific interest is the background of a man, born in Skipton, whose name is now a household word.

On the outside wall of a shop in Caroline Square is a blue slate plaque which reads:—

'This plaque was erected by the Yorkshire Society.
Thomas Spencer
Born on this site
Co-founder of
Marks and Spencer'

In 1894, Michael Marks and Israel Sieff wished to extend their business activities, and Michael Marks asked Isaac Dewhurst of Leeds, from whom he had had earlier assistance, to join him in setting up a limited company. Dewhurst declined, but instead put forward the name of his Leeds cashier, clerk, salesman and book-keeper, Thomas Spencer, who had had some twenty years experience in the drapery trade. Thomas agreed, and put up £300 against Marks' £450.

Thomas Spencer had been born in Skipton in 1851, son of John Spencer, shoemaker of Queen's Court, Skipton, and Elizabeth, his wife, formerly Elizabeth Horner of Litton. The couple had lived for some time in Bury, before moving back to their native town, and here their two eldest children were born. The youngest, Thomas, had moved to Leeds for work opportunities by the time he was 21, and there he married Elizabeth Baxter whose father was a tailor.

Thomas Spencer's grandfather had been a shoemaker in Skipton like his father, conducting business from Spencer's Yard, but he had moved to Skipton from Bradley, a village some three miles away. It seems that even earlier, in the 18th century, the Spencer family lived in Stirton, but moved to Bradley half way through the century, where they married into the Gill and Thornton families. At least one of the Spencers is described as a slater, no doubt learning his trade from the Thorntons, who had been slaters for some eight generations, and were skilled in the laying of stone slates, still to be seen in many of the older buildings, as blue slate was not used until after the coming of the railways. There are still branches of the Gill and Thornton families in Bradley. It was from the Stirton-Bradley Spencers that Thomas, co-founder of Marks and Spencer was born. Since that time, of course, the firm has expanded beyond all recognition—the Spencer contribution now only in name—but that name is on every housewife's lips, yet there has never been a branch of

Chancery Lane, demolished 1957.

Marks and Spencer in Skipton, the birth place of one of its founders.

As the population grew, so leisure pursuits became more numerous. Around 1877-8 Skipton Theatre reached it speak under the direction of W.G. Vickers. Known as the Royal Alhambra Theatre, this building stood behind the present Police Station in Otley Road.

The High Street, focus of life in the town, was a popular venue for catchpenny operators, who combined entertainment with their 'skills'. Once or twice a year, in the late 1890s, it is said that an Indian named Seequaw would put in appearance with a four-wheeled dray, which he would park outside Manby's at the end of the Middle Row. 'A bit of a band', with a trumpeter and drums was positioned on the dray, and immediately 'the band' struck up a rousing tune, attracting a curious crowd. The operator then called out in a loud and confident voice, "Painless toothpulling for a shillling!" Eventually some intrepid toothache sufferer would come tenatively forward, and be seated on a chair on the cart. Seequaw would then proceed to pull the tooth, entirely without pain-killers, but during the process the band would again strike up loudly, drowning the screams of the suffering patient! (However did Seequaw get more than the first customer?) Dentists in those days were not required to have a string of qualifications, and some were apprenticed to a master dentist in much the same way as to a butcher or joiner.

During the 19th century, coal was the fuel of industry, and the tall mill chimneys needed to be swept periodically. Mr John Atkinson was a chimney sweep in the town for 50 years. A tall chimney (demolished 1932) could be seen behind the present Woolworths' as part of the premises of William Laycock and Son, Dip and Candle Manufacturers. The firm started in 1817, and still sells agricultural requirements. Then, candles were made by repeatedly dipping wicks fastened on to metal rods into a large vat on the top floor, until the candles were of the required thickness. These candles are known to have been supplied for use in the construction of the Blea Moor Railway Tunnel on the Settle-Carlisle line.

Skipton's industry was diversified. Vanished or modified industries included once prosperous boat-building, carried on by brothers George and Jeremiah Waddington. Basket-making flourished for a time, introduced at the beginning of the 19th Century by Thomas Robinson from York, with premises in Sheep Street, and Caroline Square. There were two Skipton straw-hat manufacturers, the operatives being mainly women, and finally driven out of business by the introduction of machinery. It is known that in 1843, one Betty Airey carried on a straw-bonnet business in Chancery Lane. Tobacco and snuff were manufactured in the High Street at the beginning of the 19th Century by James and John Ward, and in the middle of the century by Thomas Kendal in Roger's Yard, and sold over the counter of a small shop in Sheep

Hardcastle's Yard

Street. It was a common sight to see Mr Kendal breaking open barrels of leaf in the main street, as the passage of his little factory was so narrow that it was impossible to run a barrel along it. At a later date 'Skipton shag' became popular in Lancashire and throughout the Yorkshire Dales. Mr George Pethybridge, traveller at that time for Wilkinson's, the makers, took packets of shag up to Aysgarth for a certain Betty Webster to smoke through her long churchwarden's pipe. Betty, in spite of her bad habits, was well over a hundred when she died.

Brewing, coach-building, clock-making and clog-making, also figure amongst once thriving industries, while John Tomlin Carter, born 1854 was a rope-maker with his works along the 'rope-walk' in the Otley Street area with entrance near the Albion Inn. At least two of his ropes were made for Skipton church bells.

The various yards and passages with which Skipton abounded at this time, might have looked quaint, but their amenities left much to be desired. In 1857 a report of the General Board of Health looked into the sanitary conditions of Hardcastle's Yard, where sixty-six cellar dwellings were recorded. It was reported that in Millfields, Middle Row and High Street, there were twelve dwellings without any privies of any kind, and in Brown's Yard there were ten families to one privy. The tenants of eight separate houses in High Street and Middle Row had to use various privies in various yards on the opposite side of the street, whereas others, even more unfortunate, had to 'go where they could'. One woman said, "We were thankful to be able to have the opportunity of going into the churchyard, but the gate is now locked!"

The 19th Century produced a few notable people connected with the town, including Richard Waller, born 1811, and famous for his paintings of old Skipton. He was reputed to have enjoyed the friendship of Dickens and Thackeray. John Dawson (1833-88) was a native of Settle, but attended Skipton Grammar School, being cashier at Dewhurst's for some 30 years, and one time proprietor of the West Yorkshire Pioneer. One of his sons, William Harbutt Dawson another ex Grammar School pupil, became a great researcher, and in 1882 published his invaluable History of Skipton. Geoffrey Robinson, born at Dyneley House in 1871, later changed his name to Dawson and became editor of the Times newspaper. A 'good' doctor, Dr Wylie also lived at this house (now demolished) and every year gave a party for the old people at his own expense.

In 1882 Charles McMoran Wilson was born in Skipton, but after four attacks of rheumatic fever in as many years, his father, a doctor, decided to move the family to more benevolent southern climes. Charles followed in his father's footsteps, took up a medical career, became Lord Moran and was for a long time personal physician to Winston Churchill. Lord Moran's ill-health

Top of Kendall's Yard, now demolished.

as an infant in Skipton did him no lasting harm, for he died at the age of 94.

As the 19th Century progressed, so the franchise was extended. Early in the century voters had to be men of substance, and in 1806 only 46 registered their votes, but since they had to travel to York, this is not surprising as some reputedly had to walk all the way. In 1834 Skipton got its own polling station, and ten years later the number of voters had risen to 141. As time went on, politics increasingly involved the common man. (Women did not get the vote until 1918). In 1885 the Conservative Club was launched in Kendall's Yard, with a memberhsip of 200, moving to Belmont Bridge four years later. (Closed 1858) Shortly afterwards the Gladstone Liberal Club was opened in premises on Mill bridge, later moving to Sackville Street. The strength of the Labour movement was still to come.

During the late 19th Century, Skipton's population rose from 6000 in 1871 to 9000 in 1891. Soon after 1900 it stood at 12,500, since which time it has remained fairly static.

On emigration to New Zealand

Towards the end of the 19th Century, times were hard in the North. There was a recession in farming, and trades generally suffered, causing many families to emigrate, seeking new lives in Canada, Australia or New Zealand.

Conditions on board ship were outlined by a former Craven resident, Mrs Anne Riley, in a letter to the father, brothers and sisters left behind. It appears that two local families, probably friends, emigrated at the same time; that is Anne with her husband, Dick, and their three children, and 'Bob' and his family. The letter was written in stages, in December 1879 on board the 'Olaki' on the way to New Zealand.

'We have now been on the water eleven weeks and five days and have nearly 2000 miles to go yet,' writes Anne. She then describes the sinking-feeling she experienced when first descending the eleven steps down into their prison-like cabin, and continues, 'Our bed is three feet wide, and it has to hold my husband, myself and Tom. Marion's bed goes across the foot of our bed, that is, our feet go under her bed. There was no room provided for baby owing to our agent not naming it on the tickets.'

The family had not expected to have to make their own meals on board, which turned out to be the case, living on food bought from the stores, mainly porridge, flour, butter, sugar, cheese, jam and tinned fish, with salt pork available twice a week. Water for drinking, cooking and washing was rationed and had to be fetched from the deck where it was pumped up from storage tanks.

'I do not know what we should have done but for the engine tenter. He is condensing water daily and is the most obliging fellow on board. I beg water off him when I wash clothes, but it is queer washing in cold water. . . I did not think my children could live so long without a fire, and there is no steam or anything to warm them. We have heat, cold, rain, hail, and snow and squalls. I used to feel frightened when I woke up in the night, and heard the sailors shouting, "Let go, and stand to your halyards!" You know when the wind alters. It sounds so confused with all the children. It's something dreadful. There are 70 children on board.'

On landing at Port Chalmers, however, 'just before Christmas' the Rileys must have perked up somewhat, for Anne records, 'The scenery is beautiful, and today is a real grand summer's day. My husband and Bob are going up to Dunedin to look for a place to live.'

Over one year later, January 26th 1880, Richard (Dick) Riley, Anne's husband, addresses a letter to his mother and family in England. By this time, the Riley family are living in rented accommodation, along with Bob and his family, and a man named Turner, all together in one house. Dick asks for a letter included to be handed to a friend 'Dixon' of Cononley, and goes on:—

'We have no furniture yet and do not intend getting any till we get some work. We have boxes for tables, boxes for chairs and beds on the floor, but the best of all is, we are in good health. Dunedin is the beautifullest city that I ever saw in my life. It has some splendid streets and nearly every house stands by itself with a piece of garden before it, and ground at the back.

But worst of all is I have got no work, but I expect some in a week or two. We have fixed up a back-stone and baked muffins and crumpets. We sold about two pounds last week and my trade has been very good here, but is very dull just at present. Plasterers have been receiving £1 a day. One plasterer told me he had earned £1 a day for the last six months and never missed a day.

Richard Riley. Post Office, Dunedin. To be called for.'

It is not known what happened to the Rileys after that, but there was an underlying note of cheerfulness and optimism in their letters in spite of initial hardships.

I am sure they made it.

V

Canal and Railway — The hey-day of the steam train

THE Leeds and Liverpool Canal preceded the railway, and became one of Skipton's main arteries. Begun in 1770, it took twenty years to complete. The first boat came through in 1773, when a section was extended to Skipton. During the next decades mills sprang up by the canal side for easy unloading of coal, and later, when Skipton expanded, and its house-building programme got under way, it was the canal that conveyed countless loads of bricks for interior walls from Lancashire.

One well-remembered name associated with the canal, is that of John Robert Thornton who owned many of the narrow boats bringing goods to the mills right up to, and after the Second War. When he retired to the Raikes area, he installed a canal-wheel-shaped gate at his home.

It was another important stage in the town's development when railway links were established in the middle of the 19th century. In 1847 the railway line to Bradford was opened, followed the next year by the line into North Lancashire, to Lancaster in 1849, and to Ilkley in 1888 (now closed past Embsay). By 1901 the line to Grassington was under construction. This only had a short life, but part of the line still runs to Swinden quarry. The rather attractive railway station, (particularly since recent cleaning has high-lighted the natural stone), was built in 1878, and there was an excellent train service. The Morecambe residential line was surprisingly busy, with trains running every day, including Sundays, and a popular Bradford-Residential business train steamed into Skipton regularly at 5.45pm, met by a bus to convey passengers to Grassington.

Skipton was on the old London, Midland and Scottish line, and could boast of being just over 200 miles from London, 40 miles from Manchester, the cotton capital, and only a few miles from the Dales borders. Such beautiful areas as Bolton Abbey, Barden Tower, Gargrave, Ilkley, Haworth, Grassington, Burnsall, Kilnsey and Kettlewell, were, and still are, within easy reach. Indeed, Skipton was an important junction until well after the Second War. There are now no direct trains from London to Skipton, (the route these days going Leeds-Carlisle) but then, the 'Thames-Forth' from St Pancras, via

Skipton Station—an old print.

Bedford and Nottingham, came directly through Skipton, and sometime in the afternoon, around 2.30, trains from either direction (London and Scotland) would meet in Skipton station, which was somewhere about half way.

Quite a number of established Skipton families 'came with the railways', some from Lancaster and the coast, others from further afield. Mr Norman Dexter, born 1916, recalls how his father originally came from Rutland, having been in the parcels office at Oakham which was on the Notts-London main line. Later he was transferred to Bradford, and finally to Skipton. Mr Dexter well remembers those hectic days when Skipton station reverberated to the thunder of the old steam trains. Hellifield station, further up the line, was then an important junction on the threshold of the scenic Settle-Carlisle route to Scotland. Hellifield still has the Blackburn line, now mainly used by goods trains and special trains for railway enthusiasts, but at one time Hellieifled was a name known to railwaymen all over the country, and at least one retired London railway worker has been known to pay a nostalgic visit to the village, simply because the name was engraved upon his memory.

During Skipton's railway hey-day before the Second War, the stationmaster for a long time was Mr Alderson, who always wore a 'boccy' (hard hat or bowler), and who lived almost 'over the shop', that is opposite the Midland Hotel, where the Fire Station now is. In his day, not only was Skipton a busy passenger line, but the station played an important role in the transporting of animals, there being three loading bays for cattle, which came from Scotland, and from Ireland via Heysham and sometimes Holyhead. In addition there was a very busy parcels office, doing as much business in a day, as in a month now. Much of the regular business was with the mills, and Irishmen would leave their bags there in haytime while they went to work on the farms.

In the Twenties there was a well-stocked Smith's bookstall on the platform, not forgetting Refreshment Rooms, where sandwiches curled up under the inevitable glass dome. As a personal touch, the booking-clerk often took a last look round to make sure that none of the 'regulars' were late, before giving the 'all-clear' for the train's departure.

In spite of what now seem to be antiquated methods, people seemed to 'manage' just as well as they do today. 'Little Johnny' for instance, had a horse-drawn cab ready to convey passengers, and 'Quake' Ingham's twowheeled truck carried a basket containing skips and clothes for commercial travellers to display at shops such as Taylor and Hannam's, drapers, of Sheep Street.

All railwaymen seemed to be good gardeners, most having allotments in the Broughton Road district, and competition was keen. Social life and sport, too, was largely connected with the railway, such as the annual Good Friday football match, 'Traffic versus Loco', when contestants played with

Parcel van outside the station.

enthusiasm for an old tin cup.

There was romance and atmosphere about the old steam trains, somehow absent in their modern counterparts. Who can ever forget those halcyon days, when as children we arrived at the station for the annual day-trip to Morecambe? What excitement as we walked up the platform looking for an empty Third Class carriage, passing on our way the driver and fireman who always seemed to be leaning out of the cab, among all the hissing and steaming! Present too, was a pungent smell of smoke and fire and oil, which only served to remind us that the delights of the sea-side were almost at hand, and we should soon be in business with the bucket and spade!

In the days of steam a railway worker's lot was more than just a job—it became a way of life—and retired engine-drivers used to talk nostalgically of their days of glory 'on the footplate'. To become an engine-driver, responsible for so many lives, meant a great deal of dedication and a long apprenticeship. It was every red-blooded boy's dream to become an engine-driver, but an aspiring driver had to learn the hard way. First he would work as a cleaner in the engine-shed to familiarise himself with every part of the engine. Then he would progress to fireman, later to driving a 'Goods' then a 'Slow' passenger train, and then—the final accolade—he graduated to become driver of an 'Express'. At the other end of the scale an ageing driver suffered the final indignity of being demoted to 'Goods' or shunting.

Old habits die hard. One octogenarian ex-Skipton engine-driver is remembered by his family for the peculiar habit he had of taking out his pocket-watch to check the time, literally every few minutes throughout the day. This was because, though then long retired, his mind and body were still geared to 'running on time'.

During the Second War the railway was of vital importance for maintaining supplies, and passenger trains were always full of uniformed personel, work-weary civilians, or sometimes prisoners-of-war with brightly coloured circles sewn on to their backs. Getting about the country depended on trains and buses, since most private cars were off the road. M.E.L. remembers, 'During the war I was working in Liverpool, and there was a most marvellous train—the 4.40pm—which ran direct to Skipton, arriving about 7.20. What a relief it was to board that train on Friday nights and escape from the bombs until Monday!

A little later I was evacuated to a remote village, five miles from the Welsh border. The wartime return journey from my home on Sundays, might be of some interest. There were no buses from Bradley to Skipton on Sunday mornings, therefore I had to get up early, and walk the three miles to Skipton, (carrying my heavy suitcase), in order to catch the morning train to Manchester. Here there was a 3½ hour wait for a connection to Chester. I then took the bus from Chester to Farndon, after which there was again no available transport, and I had no option but to walk the last five miles, (still carrying my suitcase, and making a total of eight miles of walking). I usually arrived at my destination around 8pm. Being open country, with only the odd farm or cottage here and there, understandably I got to know every stick and stone along the route of that last five weary miles. There is, however, a sequel to this story, which illustrates that truth is stranger than fiction. Long after the war we became friendly with an American couple, who made frequent visits to this country. Once, their business interests took them to Cheshire, where they rented a country cottage, and while there we were invited to visit them. Imagine my feelings of incredulity, when the cottage turned out to be one of those that I had trudged past so often on that long route-march with my suitcase, some forty years before!'

VI
Religious Life

SKIPTON'S crowning glory, is, of course, the Parish Church, Holy Trinity, situated at the top of the High Street. This building dates from the early 14th Century, but a church in various forms existed before that date. After the Dissolution, Skipton Parish Church became the burial place of the Cliffords, Earls of Cumberland, who had formerly been interred at Bolton Abbey. Of the three Skipton tombs, one was erected by Lady Anne Clifford in memory of her father, the Third Earl. In 1803 Dr Whitaker and friends obtained permission to open the tomb and found the Earl's embalmed body quite perfect, even to the mole on his face, but on exposure to air, the body crumbled to dust before their very eyes.

The church has been singularly unlucky, in that it has been struck by lightning, not once, but twice. In June 1853 lightning struck during divine service, when the west pinnacle of the tower, weighing a ton and a half, came crashing to the ground, not unnaturally unnerving the assembled congregation. Perhaps this can be expected in summer weather, but in April 1925, a thunderbolt came through the roof, causing a fire and striking the organ which was partially destroyed. It is said that it appeared to play its own funeral dirge as wierd sounds emanated from the stricken instrument, caused by hot air rushing through the pipes.

Faithful church workers contributed devoted service over long periods of time. Many will recall the late Mr Joe Wiseman who wrote the church's history, and was a capable church guide for many years. Mr Norman Mosely, a Silsden grocer, was organist at the Parish Church for 40 years (1925-65). Four men are known to have been in the choir for 50 years each—Mr Helm, grocer; Albert Armistead, pork butcher; Hector Salter, engine driver and 'Big Bill' Chew, caretaker at the library. Others who had 40-50 years service included Joe Wiseman, Bob Chew, Jim Chew and Lawson Coates. How they looked forward to their 'rewards', those annual choir trips, often to the Lakes, and usually finishing up with a sing-song in a pub!

The churchyard overlooks the High street, and even today seems strangely removed from the hustle and bustle only yards away, and is an ideal vantage point for those wishing to view the town's changing scene in comparative peace. Generally speaking, churchyards were burial places

Interior of Parish Church April 1925 after the thunderbolt and fire. Clifford Tomb in the background.

Looking down the High Street from the churchyard.

before cemeteries. In churchyards the deceased usually faced east, the clergymen, west, so that on the Day of Judgement the clerics would be ready to address their flock. As more and more graves were dug through the centuries, so the ground level in the churchyard rose, therefore as land became scarce, bodies were moved and the bones stored in a charnel house. In the 19th century, the increased population meant that many churchyards could no longer cope adequately, and this gave rise to cemeteries. Undertakers had first appeared as a profession in the 17th Century, when a wealthy deceased needed a cabinet maker for the coffin, a plumber for the lead case, and an upholsterer for the velvet fittings—but most people would be buried without these refinements. Later, Victorian funerals provided an opportunity for the family's status to be on display, when the hearse would be drawn by four black-plumed horses, and the cortège would proceed at a fittingly sombre pace until it got round the corner out of sight.

Other places of worship, though not of the same antiquity, have an equally important place in the hearts of some Skiptonians, though some are no longer in use. Still standing and in use is the old friends' Quaker Meeting House, built in 1693 down the Ginnel, then with its own cemetery.

During the 18th Century Non-Conformists began to gain a foothold, and it is known that John Wesley paid three visits to Skipton in 1764, 1766 and 1782. Wesley himself died in 1791, a member of the Church of England until the last, his aim having been to reform the established church, not necessarily to replace it. The old Wesleyan chapel at the foot of Park Hill was built about 1811, not long after his death. The Congregational Chapel was opened in 1916. By the mid-19th Century attendance at the Parish Church was full to overflowing, and so Christ Church (consecrated 1859) was built to serve the developing population, and an old map of 1860 shows it to be pleasantly located amongst green fields, (eventually to be swamped by Newtown and Middletown). Relatively quickly, other denominations began to make their appearance, until Skipton held a full complement of Methodists (Wesleyan and Primitive), Congregationalists, Christian Mission, Salvation Army, and Baptists, not forgetting the long-established Roman Catholic Church. (St Stephen's was completed in 1843) Some of these religious bodies had associated schools, having been quicker off the mark with education than the state, believing as they did, that literacy would enable children to understand the scriptures.

Many of our present day holiday breaks have religious origins. Whitsuntide was one of the outstanding events of the calendar between the wars, as recorded by Mrs Gladys Yeadon:—

'Large crowds watched the processions. Many of the female population got a new outfit or dress for 'Whit'. The Roman Catholic procession always

Skipton Parish Church (Holy Trinity).

took place on the morning of Whit Monday, culminating in a church service. Christ Church and Holy Trinity would walk at 1.30 in the afternoon, followed by the chapels, about 2.30. Hymns would be sung jointly in Caroline Square and later outside the Town Hall. The Parish church had a service in the church and then we had permission to walk through the Castle grounds, and after games and sports were held in the Rectory Fields'. (Sadly, the volume of traffic has 'put paid' to one of the year's traditional highlights).

Mrs Yeadon continues, 'As a Parish Church Sunday School scholar I took part in many processions. Mrs Dr Bob Fisher (universally referred to as 'Mrs Dr Bob') lived at the Bailey (later offices of Walker, Charlesworth and Foster). Along with a band of helpers she organised our garb on that day. A few days before, we assembled in a large first-floor room looking on to the High Street, and marvellous costumes were contrived out of yards of butter muslin in various pastel colours. Flower head-dresses were made for us, and I recall one year when each girl held either end of a flower-decked hoop or arch. A lot of work must have been done in the morning, if real. The procession started on the early afternoon headed by the Parish Church Choir (in surplices) and clergy, followed by Sunday School scholars, the little ones perched on forms in carts supervised by their teachers.' (Mrs Barbara Mason recalls that one cart always came from Niffany Farm, and had sheep gates round the edge and was trimmed with foliage).

'The Christ Church contingent was next, followed by all the many (in those days) Non-Conformist churches. I think the Salvation Army made up the rear. I can't remember the starting off point, but we ended up parading up the High Street, and into the church for a service. The church was always packed, and hymns such as 'Onward Christian Soldiers' rendered double force!

The next item was a decorous walk, in 'crocodile' round the Castle grounds, then tea in whichever Sunday School one attended. For Parish Church scholars the day was rounded off by sports in the Rectory Field which lay between the Rectory and Overdale and is now the site of Mr Tom Clarke's house.'

Ermysted's Grammar School Form—early 20th Century.

VII
The Forward March of Education

SKIPTON is rightly proud of Ermysted's Boys' Grammar School, which has produced so many scholars and men who have made their mark in many spheres of life, and which has managed to survive as a Grammar School up to the present day. It was in 1548 that the school was re-founded by William Ermysted, who became Canon of St. Paul's, and from whom it takes its name.

In its early days the Grammar School always had a close association with the Church. Indeed, in 1727, John Wesley even toyed with the idea of taking up an appointment as teacher there. He was attracted by the prospect of a good salary and living a hard life in 'this frightful town,' but the position never materialised. The first Ermysted's School was kept in a house in Newmarket Street, and the scholars attended from 6am to 6pm in summer, with a 2-hour break at mid-day, and from 7am to 6pm in winter. In 1877 it moved to its present position in a new building up Gargrave Road, where it still operates, although there have been numerous additional buildings and refinements through the years.

In the early 20th Century there was a proportion of fee-paying scholars, but 'Scholarship' children were also its life-blood. County Minor Scholarships were 'sat' at the age of 10-12, and children who failed the first time could try again the following year. Because Skipton is the 'capital' of a far-flung rural area, the Grammar School provided accommodation for boarders, some coming from villages and isolated farms up the Dales.

Mr Tom Yeadon of Litton, who for many years was Engineer and Surveyor to Skipton Rural District Council, has memories of School House at Ermysted's where he was a boarder in the early 20s. He records:

'Attendance at Skipton Parish Church for Matins and Evensong was obligatory, plus 8am Communion Service (monthly) after Confirmation. The boys walked from school to church in a 'crocodile', the younger boys wearing Eton collars and short jackets, referred to as 'bum-freezers'. About the age of 14 or 15 they progressed to suits, that is black jackets, waistcoats and dark grey trousers. Caps were worn in summer and 'straw bens' in summer. On Sunday afternoons pupils went for a formal walk, supervised by monitors of prefects. The boys returned to what the matron called a 'plain sweet tea' which consisted of bread and butter only. Jam or cake was produced from a boy's own

Miss Broadbent, former headmistress of the Girls' High School, on the occasion of her 80th birthday, with Miss Bertha Peacock, then president of the Old Girls' Guild.

'tuck-box'. (Shades of Greyfriars and Billy Bunter!).

Written permission, signed by a housemaster or monitor, was required before a boy was allowed 'down-town', that is into Skipton, and the purpose of the excursion had to be specified, such as 'shopping' or a visit to the dentist's. A barber attended School-house periodically to cut the boys' hair. In the Twenties he was Mr Gill, whose shop was situated between the Craven Herald and the Black Horse. Incidentally, one of his grandsons was P.E. master at Ermysted's in the Sixties.'

A number of private schools became established in Skipton, including St. Monica's Convent, founded in 1867, and endowed by Monica Tempest, but this educational establishment, much respected between the wars, is now no more.

A name to be revered in Skipton was that of Sylvestor Petyt (1640-1719) who was a principal of Barnard's Inn in 1701, and who founded the Petyt Charity. Money from this source benefitted education in the town, and many ex-pupils of the Girls' High School will recall having to learn by heart the inscription above the stairs in the old building, of which, lurking in the memory, remain the words, 'Qui s'estime Petyt deviendra grand'.

The Girls' High School started life in 1886 in the Temperance Hall, Sackville Street, where Miss Larner was the first headmistress with about 40 pupils in her care, while a purpose-built school was being completed up Gargrave Road. This opened in 1890 as the Girls' Endowed School. Miss Larner was followed by Miss Broadbent, who in turn was followed by Miss Wise in 1931. In the early part of the century the school also had a fee-paying kindergarten, taught by Miss Winch (of the fuzzy hair), and attended by small boys, most of whom later graduated to the Boys' Grammar School, a little further down the road. The Girls' School also had to serve a large rural area, and accommodated a number of pupils from Lancashire and other parts of the country, and eventually there were three boarding houses, the School House, West Bank and the Hostel, the last two being across the road. Large numbers of children travelled in daily from surrounding villages, and many others came in from Barnoldswick and Earby, travelling on the now defunct railway line. (By the 1930s the number of pupils at the G.H.S had risen to the region of 500).

The School set great store by academic achievement, and aimed also to turn out 'young ladies' on whom, hopefully, in matters of speech and decorum, it had set its stamp, (though I am afraid we did sometimes let the side down!). Again, during the 30s there were both fee-paying (£3 a term) and scholarship children. Entry to the professions in those days around Skipton was mainly through the Grammar Schools, and if you fell at the first fence (County Minor), there were then fewer opportunities to 'make good' academically. At that time pupils at most other schools left at the age of 14, as these

Stone Laying at Water Street School 1890.

schools were not equipped for sixth form work or School Certificate or Matriculation examinations.

Pupils at the Girls' School wore the now old-fashioned 'gymn-slips', and because of all the trekking about between buildings, to 'forget' to change from outdoor to indoor shoes was a most heinous and punishable crime! Girls wore velvety velour hats in winter, and white straw Panamas in summer, both complete with head-bands, and both vulnerable to weather conditions, when rain reduced the sleek velvet to spotted felt, and white Pamamas turned into yellow 'lids' with corrugated brims.

Meanwhile, elementary schools in Skipton had been increasing to meet the towns needs. Throughout the 19th Century, but particularly in the latter half, most of Skipton's schools were built, some denominational, others 'Board' and later 'Council' schools. Building continued into the 20th Century, with Brougham Street Council School built in 1909, and Ings School 1911, while mid-way through the century Greatwood Primary School was opened to cater for children living in new estates erected near what was once Cawder Ghyll Isolation Hospital.

Today (1990) the Grammar Schools have managed to survive against all odds, and are still giving a first-class education, whilst Aireville Secondary School, opened since the war, too, has many opportunities and facilities to offer. Children now have many more avenues of further education, and academics and employers no longer care as much whether or not a child went to the Grammar School, but rather what results have been achieved. Those who apply themselves, but who would at one time have been denied further opportunity, now regularly go on to become achievers. This can only be a good thing.

Marriage and other 'unseemly conduct'

Teaching is today a much more difficult occupation than is generally realised, but if we need to remind ourselves just how much things have changed, the following extract taken from a West Riding County Education Schools Bulletin, speaks for itself. Conditions in England were also Spartan (as evidenced by the writer's grandmother, headteacher of a small Craven village school at this date), where similar conditions to those below applied.

In 1872 a New York School Principal set out the following rules for teachers.

'1. Teachers will each day fill lamps, clean chimneys (i.e. of lamps), and trim wicks.

2. Each teacher will bring a bucket of water and shuttle of coal for the day's session.

SKIPTON
Brougham St.
Council St.
St. III 1910

3. Make your pens carefully. You may whittle nibs to the individual taste of the pupil.
4. Men teachers may take one evening each week for courting purposes. (!)
5. After 10 hours in school the teacher may spend the remaining time reading the Bible or other good book.
6. Women teachers who marry or engage in other unseemly conduct will be dismissed. (!)
7. Every teacher should leave aside from each pay a goodly sum of his earnings for his benefit during his declining years, so that he will not be a burden on society.
8. Any teacher who smokes, uses liquor in any form, frequents Pool or public halls or gets shaved in a barber's shop will give good reason to suspect his worth, intentions, integrity and honesty.'

Opposite page:

Brougham Street School 1910.

Row 1 (back). John Spence, Fred Peacock, Billy Harvey, Harold Girling, Edgar Pilling, Eric Hall, Albert Aldersley, John W. Wittingham, Harry Alderson, Tom Stratton

Row 2. Arthur Townsend, — , Kenneth Holmes, Percy Driver, Sam Lofthouse, — Foley, — Hawkeswell, Clarence Haigh, Alfred Charnley, — , — Lilley

Row 3. D. Woodrup, Bessie Armstrong, Elizabeth Benson, Annie I'Anson, Edith Hutchinson, Gladys Watson, Evelyn Thornton, Myra Smith, Mona Lister, Madge Hargreaves

Row 4. Elsie Whitham, Kathleen Bell, Ella Gill, Sarah J. Ideson, Sarah J. Ideson, Elsie Foulds, Mona Greenwood, Ivy Clark, Elizabeth Wallbank, Jessie Jackson

Row 5. Harry Johnson, Reuben Ideson, Fred Baines, Verlie Foulds, Alice Knowles, Evelyn Peacock, Harry Riley, Ronald Hall, John Riley.

Back of the Red Lion Hotel.

VIII
Taverns in the town

AS SKIPTON was a market town, it abounded with inns, and a list of former hostelries as they were towards the end of the 19th Century is to be found in poetry form in Dr Rowley's book 'Old Skipton'. Inns were more than mere drinking houses, though they fulfilled that function too. Basically, they catered for travellers, providing food and accommodation, warmth and company, most of them having stabling for horses in a yard at the back. Many inns were also farms, with shippons and land attached. Moreover, the very names of old 'pubs' usually tells us a good deal about the local history of a town and its environs.

When in 1906 cattle disappeared from the Skipton streets, the Skipton pubs began to go into a decline—no one then being able to foresee the current tourist boom brought about by jet flight and motorways. (Incredible as it may seem, there were no motorways until after the Second War). These inns would have helped to preserve the atmosphere of the old market town, but during the demolition craze after the war many of them were pulled down and have gone beyond recall, while others were incorporated into estate agent's offices, clubs and similar premises. The Working Men's Club at the bottom of Castle Street, for instance, is said to have been an inn—now only the tell-tale archway gives a clue as to its former use.

The oldest inn which still survives up the 'Street' is reputedly the Red Lion, possibly dating back for 500 years, and the Black Horse on the opposite side is a 17th Century building built on a more historic site. Erected in 1676, it was once an ale-house known as the King's Head, and tradition has it that here were located the mews of King Richard III from 1483 to 1485. The elegant Devonshire Hotel survives at the entrance to Newmarket Street, and once provided accommodation for stage-coach travellers using the old turnpike road up Short Bank Road and over the moor to Ilkley and York. The King's Arms was sadly demolished in 1968, although an inn had reputedly stood on the spot for 350 years. The Cock and Bottle still adds a bit of almost rural charm—if you look for it—in an otherwise unexciting Swadford Street.

In the 19th Century hops were added to the brewing process and 'beer' replaced traditional ale. Gin drinking posed a real problem in the early 1800s, when conditions in urban areas were so appalling, and a great deal of cheap gin was consumed as a way of assuaging despair. In 1830 the authorities, alarmed by the scale of the problem, introduced the Beer Houses Act. By this, anyone who handed over £2 could get a licence to sell beer, but not spirits, which were taxed more heavily. As a result the nation was weaned away from gin, and beer became the national drink. Back-street beer houses proliferated. Beer was served from jugs in the kitchen, known as the Tap Room, and other rooms were opened as Snugs or Smoking Rooms. Next, purpose-built pubs began to appear, and at one time beer was drunk almost universally by hospital patients, by industrial workers who drank it to replace sweat. Even children drank beer.

A true story is recorded of a 19th Century Skipton Church Sunday School trip, when children were said to be rolling about 'fresh' on the tombstones, while their more privileged teachers sipped tea!

Beer drinking caused almost as big a problem as the gin drinking had done, and so the Temperence Movement began, and Refreshment Rooms, Temperence Bars and Coffee Taverns sprang up.

Skipton's Coffee Tavern stood towards the top end of Sheep Street almost opposite Manby's. In the early Twenties, it was lit by gas-light, and in the dim light still seemed to belong to the Victorian era. Here brass token coins to the value of 1d, 2d and 3d had been issued to farm workers to ensure that they actually got value in meals instead of liquid refreshments, but these tokens were not used after 1910.

Today few inns remain up Skipton's High Street, and with their demise went a few more of the town's links with the past.

IX
The Great War 1914-1918

UNTIL the 20th Century which spanned two worlds wars, battles were largely fought by professionals and did not involve the bulk of the population. Hardly anything in recorded history can match up to the slaughter and sacrifice occasioned by First World War, and the England (and Skipton) described was the England for which so many fought and died. Skipton's War Memorial stands in the front of the Church at the top of the High Street and replaced the statue of Sir Matthew Wilson which is now in front of the library. Millions of graves in France and indeed all over the world, bear witness to the fallen, and military cemeteries continue to be tended with loving care by the War Graves Commission, which has done, and is doing, a wonderful job. Many local men were among the thousands who died on the Somme, but when France was again overrun in the Second War, the First War Cemeteries fell into rack and ruin. After the war they were once more restored to their former immaculate condition. As the years go by there are fewer and fewer visitors directly connected with the Somme, but the cemeteries are cared for just the same, whether containing thousands of graves, or only a few dozens—men perhaps buried where they fell, and now in the middle of a ploughed field. Known graves are easy to locate, merely by writing to the War Graves Commission, who will supply all possible information. The cemeteries are well signposted, and in each are wall recesses containing two books, one listing the graves, the other a visitors' book. The visitors' books contain comments such as 'This must never happen again', 'What a tragic waste of life', and so on, for even after so many decades he would be hard-hearted indeed who did not supress a tear when confronted by the mass evidence of a generation's sacrifice. One wondered sometimes, 'How do the native French people feel?' surrounded as they are by so many English cemeteries as well as their own. Some, at least, pause to think, as evidenced by a comment entered in one book by a French person, obviously with little command of the English language, but who had struggled to put his thoughts into words. With some poignancy, he wrote:-

'Remembrances of braves British soldiers
Deads for we'

Along with the rest of the nation, Skipton played its part, and there is a story

First War Soldiers lined up for departure from Skipton Station. Many would not return.

behind every name on every memorial.

Sometimes there seemed to be neither rhyme nor reason in determining who should live, and who should die. For example, William Milne, a World War 1 'Tommy' used to tell how, when fighting in the trenches, very young men were sometimes sent up the line as replacements. It was often necessary to go out at night into 'No Man's Land' (between British and German lines) for water or to reconnoitre. On one occasion, he and another soldier had a young lad with them, and so they walked in single file, treading carefully in case of hidden mines, with the boy between them for his protection. Then the enemy started shelling, and the youth was killed, but the men survived. Another time it was the job of the Royal Engineers to clear a minefield, where the mines had been laid strictly in a pattern, One young soldier deviated by an inch or two, detonated a mine, and was blown up, only his pocket book remaining intact. On another occasion the R.E.s entered a deserted village which had been shelled and occupied by the Germans. It was a sobering experience to enter one house which was in complete ruins, apart from a crucifix left untouched on the mantlepiece.

In retrospect, the war had its lighter moments. The late Mr George Bradley, when in the R.A.M.C. was assistant to a dentist at Le Havre which was the railhead for the Front, where Chinese Labour Battallions loaded the trains. When a Chinaman had a toothache it was George's job to coat the tooth with iodine, and hold the man down as the tooth was being extracted. Often the Chinaman would jump straight up in the air, shouting, "No welleee goodee. La!"

Richard Stott's Journal

Richard Stott, formerly of 9, King Street, Skipton, was one of the few private soldiers of the Great War who recorded his experiences as a Prisoner-of-War. Here are extracts from his journal, reproduced by kind permission of the curator of the Craven Museum, Mrs Mansergh.

Private Stott, of the Duke of Welington's Regiment, describes how, when convalescing after an operation in France, word came through that the Germans had started a big 'push', and all men fit enough, be they cooks, clerks or bandsmen, were ordered to Benthan to dig trenches in an attempt to stem the advancing tide.

'Now it began to get dark. . . our eyes forever looking forward into the night thinking we could see some shadowy form. As day broke, all hell seemed to be let loose and the attack started, rifles, machine guns and artillery, firing point blank. On and on they came, just like a football match loosing. To escape now would mean certain death.'

Pte Stott continued to describe how the sergeant, also from Skipton, (unfortunately not named) was a good leader, giving orders such as, ''Give 'em 'ell, lads.'' By now rifles were red hot and full of grit and dirt from the shells dropping all around. Richard admits to saying his prayers many times during this life-and-death situation, but eventually, there being no alternative, the Tommies threw up their hands as the Germans pounced. This was the start of his experiences as a Prisoner-of-War.

At first, things turned out better than expected. The Germans were little more than boys, and one said to them ''Come, Tommy, come,'' at the same time handing out chocolate and asking for souvenirs. 'He who had been an enemy a few moments ago, now seemed like a friend.' They were still under intense fire, and 'Fritz' was carrying a Mills Bomb, which the British lads eyed warily, expecting that at any moment he would say, ''Share this among you!'' or its equivalent. Instead, however, he led the prisoners safely into a deep shell-proof shelter, complete with telephone, seats and tables—and curious glances from other Germans inside.

When the bombardment had eased off, the prisoners were marched en bloc, passing many dead and wounded on the way—both horses and men. In time they arrived at a camp in Belgium, where some two thousand other prisoners were congregated, including many from Skipton. One soldier remarked. ''By Gum, I bet t'Pioneer'll be full of prisoners this week!'' At the same time they thought of the folks back home, and who would soon be getting the news, 'Your son is reported missing. . . .' The boys at the camp longed for a smoke, (this was before the anti-smoking campaign), and consequently there was a rush for the stubs dropped by German sentries, but some of the more sadistic 'just jumped on them, and smiled.'

The prisoners were told that they were to be sent to Germany where they would be treated well, but this turned out to be a false assumption, and from then on their fortunes declined. Instead, driven like a flock of sheep, unwashed and unshaved, they arrived at the dreaded 'Black Hole of Lille', where the men were herded into dungeon-like cells, each about 8 yards by 25 yards, and with 250 men to a cell. Only one small barred window provided ventilation and daylight to this stinking hole. There were no lavatories, but at the end of each cell a large iron bowl had to suffice. All the prisoners could do, was to look forward to tomorrow, when with a bit of luck, the soup might be a bit less watery!

After three weeks the lads were marched off again, and Pte Stott describes how the fresh French air smelled 'fair grand' after the Black Hole of Lille. Then followed a spell of working on railway sidings, unloading hay and straw, when unsympathetic German guards continually goaded them with words that sounded like 'Loose, loose arbeit.' (Hurry, hurry, work) Next the prisoners were sent to Lomme, a village between Lille and Armentières (of Mademoiselle from 'Marmetiers' fame). Here they were billeted in shell-shattered houses, and set to work unloading barges, mending roads, or preparing landing ground for aircraft, while living mainly on soup and coffee from ground burnt acorns.

Eventually their journey to the Fatherland began, when they were herded into loose boxes, the journey broken by stops at evil-smelling camps and rat-infested huts. At last, on July 18th after three months of capture, they arrived in Dolmen, Germany. In vain Richard Stott conjured up mental pictures of 'dear old England', but no news came from home, largely because of all the moving about to which they were subjected. At Dolmen, a German doctor passed all men as fit with the words "Good grubba." On hearing this, their hopes soared, only to be dashed when they discovered that 'grubba' meant mines, not food, and they were indeed destined to work in iron-ore mines at Metz in Alsace-Lorraine. Here there were also some five hundred Russian prisoners, and the Britishers were detailed to work in pairs—sometimes with a Russian companion—on 12-hour shifts. Working conditions and food here were so bad that the prisoners became thoroughly selfish, owing to the instinct for survival. Pte Stott himself, lost three stones in weight, and at last, pronounced unfit for work was sent to Sneveringden, where he had a welcome shave, wash and change of underclothing. The sergeant, from Skipton, advised him, "Whatever tha does, stick to thi tablets o' soap, and don't part wi' 'em for nowt!" (Sadly, at a later stage Pte Stott had to do a deal even for this precious commodity).

A kindly guard then took him to work on a farm, where he had his own bed-sitting room, and each morning there was a knock at the door, accompanied by, "Come, Englander, come coffee drinking." Dinner might be potatoes, carrots, beans, cabbage, barley and apples all in one large pan together, which they ladled out, helping themselves. When he recovered and became stronger, he was sent back to Sneveringden, and later to a camp half-full of Italian prisoners, where they sang Italian songs alternating with 'I'ts a long way to Tipperary'—and living on frog soup.

It was while in this camp that the Armistice was signed. 'We just went daft, and jumped about like happy schoolboys, singing until early morning, and swearing we would no longer work for the Germans. Next morning came the familiar, "Loose, loose, arbeit," but not a man moved, in spite of being slashed with whips and prodded with bayonets. So it was a case of 'no work, no rations,' although the 'I-ties' managed to find a few frogs and potatoes salvaged from a ploughed field.' Told they were to be sent home, their hopes were dashed when they found themselves in 'yet another dirty, filthy camp, where there were prisoners of all nationalities, soldiers, civilians, men, women and children, the children dressed in sacks, as they had been born while their mothers were in prison.'

All this time there had been no news from home,'but at last an English officer came along distributing the first and last food parcel, comprising jam sandwiches, Irish stew and cigarettes.' A miserable Christmas Day came and went, and on Boxing Day the men were moved to Hamlyn, where once again they met up with many pals from Skipton. By this time Pte. Stott's uniform was somewhat unorthodox, as he sported a French cap, English torn tunic, a pair of Italian riding breeches, and high-top German boots, At last the journey home began, and after a hostile farewell to the 'Englanders' from German children en route, they arrived in Enshede, Holland, where a great welcome awaited them, and where they were fed, cleaned up, and generally treated like heroes.

Then on to Hull. 'As we drew near hooters from other ships sounded as we sighted land, where a band played on the quay, on 1st January 1919. Then train to Ripon to be demobbed, and then Home, Sweet Home.'

Pte Stott concluded that there were good and bad amongst all nationalities. Generally, it seemed that the smaller the numbers, the better the treatment. The treatment always deteriorated when men were herded together in large numbers, and personal contact was lost. The war experiencies remained with the soldiers all their lives. Richard Stott, himself, settled down once again in his home town of Skipton, and resumed his old job as a weaver, later working in the signal and telegraph department of the railway. He died at the age of 79.

X
The Rural Community

UNTIL after the Second War, Skipton castle owned much of the land in the neighbourhood, and it was not until 1956 that this was sold off on a large scale. Prior to that, many local farmers had been tenants of the Castle, although they had had a good measure of independence for some time, and through difficult periods had become well used to paddling their own canoes. Skipton's geographical position meant that for years it had been a centre for farming activities. A certain amount of corn was once grown in Craven, but ideal conditions for the drying of grain only came round about once in every seven years, and inevitably there were catastrophic crop failures from time to time. Severe famines were recorded in 1795 and 1812 when steps had to be taken to provide corn, potatoes and other provisions at reduced prices to avoid starvation.

From an early date there was a corn market up the High Street, and corn dealers flocked to the town from all parts of adjoining counties. Skipton stood between York and Lancaster, and on Saturdays large amounts of grain were brought in from the other side of Blubberhouses, where the atmosphere is less damp, and then dispersed to Craven and North East Lancashire. It is said that in the early 1800s some two hundred carts attended the weekly market. Now, with modern transport facilities, corn growing has been wisely left to those parts of the country with a dryer atmosphere, which is why our Craven countryside is today so beautifully green, unspoilt by ploughed fields.

Although Skipton's name was derived from sheep, cattle have long played a part in the town's farming history. Many locals are familiar with old paintings or prints depicting an enormous peculiarly square-shaped cow, the famous 'Craven Heifer'. This wondrous animal, a four-year old Shorthorn, was exhibited in the early 1800s. Bred and fed by the Revd W Carr on one of His Grace the Duke of Devonshire's estates at Bolton Abbey, she weighed 312 stones (8lbs to a stone), and was the largest and fattest cow ever shown in England. Teams of horses conveyed her from one town to another on show, visiting Bradford, Wakefield, Pontefract, Doncaster and Rotherham, then on to London, Chesterfield., Alfreton, Ripley, Derby, Loughborough, Leicester, Northampton, Newport, Dunstable, St. Albans and finally Smithfield, a truly remarkable feat of organisation in itself. Ladies and gentleman were charged

The Pinfold where stray cattle were impounded by the pinder. The old building behind is a 17th century brewhouse, converted into flats by Mrs M.D. Wales, architect.

one shilling to view, but servants got away with sixpence.

As Skipton developed it became a great market for both cattle and sheep. About 1809 a fortnightly fair was being held up the 'Street' (High Street), when sheep pens were set up and pigs roamed about the town. Many Lancashire dealers attended this fair, held on alternate Tuesdays throughout the year. How busy the High Street would be as cattle were bought and sold, farmers and dealers bargaining and socialising, and the many public houses doing a roaring trade. By 1886, however, change was on the horizon, when Messrs Throup and Davis opened an auction mart near the railway station. Some cattle must still have continued to be sold in the streets, because later the same year at a farmers' meeting proposals were discussed to open another cattle market, in order to remove cattle from the streets altogether. It was not until 1906, twenty years later, that the cattle were finally moved into open-air cattle pens in Jerry Croft. It seems, therefore, that although the auction mart was operating down Broughton Road, Irishmen and others continued to sell in the streets for some time, (probably to avoid paying commission) and then carried on trading in Jerry Croft until this space was needed for a car park. Thereafter all official business was conducted down Broughton Road. Trading in the town centre had constituted a considerable nuisance, and the iron railings round trees planted to celebrate Queen Victoria's Diamond Jubilee in 1897 afforded some measure of protection. The removal of the cattle dealt a blow to the once thriving hostelries of the town. Most old public houses had stabling, shippons and even land attached, but now as business declined, many were closed down. A few survived, and there are some farmers who remember big shippons behind the Old George and the Royal Oak in use as recently as the Second War.

Between the wars, certain Irish dealers, such as Francis O'Brian, Keenan and McNally, came over regularly to sell Irish dairy cattle and stores (for fattening). The cattle had had a rough passage from Ireland, and were accompanied by drovers who were required to keep the beasts on their feet all the time in transit, because had they fallen over while in a rocking boat they would never have got up again. Francis had two men working for him. He would get hot water from the pubs, and pour it into large barrels situated round the back. To this he added quantities of bran and brown sugar, the resulting mixture being ladled out into buckets for the cows. Some dealers would add salt to the feed the day before the sale, so that thirsty cows would be ready to drink, would fill out, and would be looking their best for the market. All Irish cattle had to have a licence to guard against Foot and Mouth disease, and were then quaranteened for about 28 days on the farms after sale. Many of the Irishmen were heavy drinkers, and are remembered as hard bargainers, who would argue long and hard over a shilling. They probably

Cattle Trading in the High Street.

The Cattle Market, Jerry Croft—now a car park.

introduced the curious custom of 'luck money', which exists to this day, much to the perplexity of first-time buyers from the South. (For with modern-day transport Skipton's trade has extended further afield). What 'luck' amounts to, is that after a sale the buyer gives an agreed amount of money back to the vendor 'for luck'—in effect a sort of unofficial discount. Deals were struck literally by the striking of hands.

Well-known English dealers were Ben Chester of Bradley, Wrathalls and Harrisons, sometimes bringing Ayrshire Shorthorn Cross animals down from Scotland by train. Between the wars there were fewer cattle wagons and many more drovers would walk cattle from one place to another. Cattle could be seen flowing down Broughton Road up to the beginning of the second war. Besides cattle, an annual Cattle Horse Fair used to be held in Skipton early in the century when horses were run up and down the High Street, while dealers assessed their capabilities.

The hilly Craven landscape lent itself to fairly small mixed farms, but as time went by, more acres of rough land were cultivated, although thankfully large tracts of moorland still remain with a scenic beauty second to none. Early methods of land improvement can be seen in the lime-kilns dotted about in fields where limestone was once burnt for spreading on land in order to break up and sweeten the soil. The Skipton district is founded partly on limestone and partly on millstone grit, so that even in sandstone areas, lime is never very far away.

Between the wars, and indeed until just after the Second War, lots of farms were still worked by horses and the tractor was an innovation. After the First War many horses came on to the market, most of which had been branded with red-hot irons. Some of these animals were highly temperamental and difficult to manage as farm horses, having suffered their own baptism of fire in France. Ben Lancaster remembers one ex-war horse that could not be restrained from whipping at speed round every corner, almost taking the wall with it.

Since the Second War farming methods all over the country have been revolutionised, and Craven is no exception. Modern farms look more like factories with buildings taking up an enormous amount of space. Small farms that used to support families have disappeared altogether, the land having been put to other farms. Surplus traditional farm-houses with grey-slated roofs and mullioned windows have become trendy residences for commuters from the city. The use of chemical fertilizers has increased tremendously, boosting production, but who knows at what cost? Put it down to looking through rose-coloured spectacles if you like, but in the 20s and 30s there really did seem to be a different 'feel' about the fields and meadows. Buttercups, daisies, cowslips and marguerites blew about in the wind, and on a warm summer's evening the air was filled with the scent of new-mown hay, honeysuckle, and the indefinable aroma of assorted wild flowers. In the woodlands we picked blue-bells, celandines, marsh marigolds and anemones, and the stream ran clear as we cupped our hands to drink, without a thought of any form of pollution.

Until the post-war era of mechanisation and chemical fertilizers, most farms were run as family concerns, and women and children were expected to help out (unpaid) so as to eke out a living. This involved working all the hours that God sends during haytime, in order to provide feed for the coming winter. Extra help came in the shape of Irish labourers who would gather around the Skipton High Street pubs on Mondays, from late June to early July, seeking to be hired for a month's haymaking, (some of them having taken French leave from building sites up and down the country). Farmers, too, would congregate in small knots, trying to spot a likely lad, and eventaully a tentative approach would be made. After a bit of hard bargaining the Irishman would agree upon a wage for the month—sometimes as high as £5! plus his 'keep', (or even £50 at one time—but this was big money in those days). It was tacitly agreed that the man would work all hours, even to midnight, in good weather, but was free to go before the end of the month should haytime be finished. This did happen or rare occasions, but more often than not, one wet week followed another, and the Irishman was set to work stubbing thistles or cleaning out shippons. Quite often he departed at the end of the month leaving most of the hay still to be gathered and the farmer with a big hole in his pocket. Sometimes, Irishmen came back year after year to the same farm, almost as family friends. Others were good workers, but 'took a fair bit of handling' as one farmer put it.

Most farmers were milk producers, and even a small farm with about twenty milk cows, plus a few sheep, pigs and hens, would have a 'farmer's man' living in. (Farmers then did not keep more stock than the land would sustain and today's vast herds were not possible before the Second War). The farmer's man would be hired by the year at Lancaster, Settle or Kendal 'Hirings'. The standard wage about 1930, was £1 per week, plus a man's 'keep'! For that he was expected to rise early, work most of the week-end, and get up in the night if necessary to help attend a calving cow or farrowing pig. One farmer's man in my youth asked father permission to have Saturday morning off. This was refused, whereupon the man protested, "Asslatta 'ev it off, boss. I'm getting wed!" Surprisingly, from their small wages many a farm man was able to realise his dream of one day farming on his own account, even if his first farm had to be somewhere at the back of the beyond.

M.E.L. recalls. 'On our farm at Bradley, my father and his man would get up about 4.30am, and after hand-milking the cows (using paraffin storm-

W. Anderton, Skipton Vet.

lamps for illumination in winter), the milk would be taken by horse and float to catch the 7.30am train to Leeds from Cononley Station'. This sort of thing applied all over the Dales, and milk regularly went by train to London from Hawes.

There was in those days no Milk-Marketing Board, and whatever problems the modern farmer has, marketing this perishable commodity is not one of them. Up to the early 1930s and the appearance of the M.M.B. the farmer was responsible for selling his own milk wholesale, and usually had a retail outlet in the city, such as Bradford or Leeds. Sometimes a fickle retailer would give a week's notice, at the end of which time the farmer found himself feeding, not only his family, but all his cows as well. In such an emergency, out came the separator and hand-operated churn, and the farmer's wife then had no option but to set to making butter—a long and laborious job. The finished product would next have to be hawked around the village, while her husband tramped unfamiliar city streets desperately looking for another 'milk shop'. With a bit of luck, this might materialise after a number of weeks, and then the butter-making would be thankfully abandoned.

Milk was delivered locally in Skipton by roundsmen. Between the wars, and just after, milk costing 4d a pint was delivered twice a day, and before the days of bottling, was put into almost anything on the doorstep, jam jars, basins, vases, jugs. George Throup remembers the same ring of custard on the same jug for three weeks, until in the end he had to say, "Nay, missus. Let's have a clean jug!" (These sort of customers were usually the ones to complain about milk going sour in summer). As with beer, a gill of milk meant half a pint. Not a lot of families had bathrooms at this time, and it was not uncommon to deliver milk and find the occupant of the house in the old tin bath in front of the fire!

At one time half the milk-rounds in Skipton were owned by the Marshall family, Bertha (Mrs Swindlehurst) delivering milk for no less than 50 years.

Few farmers ever had a holiday. They now travel abroad like everybody else, drive smart cars, and often live in modernised houses, a far cry from the universally stone-flagged kitchens, cold water taps, stone sinks and side-ovens. Though as smart as anyone when 'dressed up', a working farmer could often be identified by a piece of band (string) tied round a tattered raincoat, prone as he was to catching clothing on nails and barbed wire. I am reminded of an observant little girl from a Lancashire town, holidaying in Bradley many years ago, who suddenly turned to my father and said, "Mr Throup Why DO farmers always wear ragged coats?"

Farming was a hard life, but there were many compensations. Often a few farms would be grouped together in the small villages or hamlets of Craven, and rarely would one farmer see another 'stuck fast' in times of illness,

Niffany Farm.

adversity, or even routine pressure of work. At dipping time or clipping time, for instance, the farming fraternity would often join together to help one another. Where today there is only one farm, perhaps once there were four or more. The redundant farm houses might look a good deal smarter now that they are occupied by well-heeled commuters, but something of intrinsic value has gone out of rural life, and it seems unlikely that it will return.

Workers at the old Silk Mill (Low Mill, Sackville Street) taken one dinnertime. Back row. left. Cissie Storey (Mrs Tom Smith), Bell Storey (Mrs Kendall), Florrie Shorter (Mrs Hepworth), Alice Dobney, John W. Hallam, Ivy Robinson, Eleanor Ford. Front row. Florrie Marsden (Mrs Bryant), Setta Atkinson, Miss Boothman (Mrs Armistead), Ruth Tillotson (Mrs Barrett).

XI
Skipton's Manufacturing Industry

ON ACCOUNT of locally grown wool, hand loom weaving was one of Skipton's principle occupations and some houses were three-storey, with handloom weaving on the top floor. But as time went by, with the advent of power looms, and canal and rail transport, Skipton's industry developed more along the lines of Lancashire's, with silk and cotton predominating. The cotton industry became established in the Pennine district because the brittle cotton threads did not snap easily in the damp atmosphere.

On the Lancashire approach to the town, the chief landmark is still Belle Vue Mill, built in 1828 by John Dewhurst for worsted spinning and weaving, but rebuilt in 1831 after a fire as a cotton mill. The Dewhursts had been farmers at Marton, where Thomas Dewhurst furthered his interest in sheep by also trading in wool, ultimately supplying suitable 'twist' to handloom weavers in Dales farmhouses and cottages. In late 1798, Thomas bought a building at Elslack, (Mill Cottage), and this he converted into a small mill for cotton spinning by water power. Later various other properties were acquired, two at Millholme near Skipton, Scalegill near Malham, and the Old Soke Mill at Airton, culminating in the building of the aforementioned Belle Vue in 1828.

The introduction of steam power was not without its traumas, for handloom weavers were fearful for their livelihoods. There were serious riots in 1826 and 1842, when large mobs from Burnley and Colne advanced up on the town with the object of drawing plugs from boilers in the mills, so putting fires out and stopping production. Rioters managed to draw plugs at Messrs Dewhurst and Sidgwicks of High Mill, but were eventually confronted by mounted Hussars. John Settle, a shrewd old timber merchant became alarmed when business in Skipton was suspended and shops and houses locked and bolted. He therefore pretended to sympathise with the mob, offering the use of a field and the loan of a wagon to carry away food which had been stolen for sustenance. This was merely a ruse to draw the mob into open country where they could be dispersed by soldiers. No shots were fired, but one soldier was killed by a stone, and Mr Garforth of Coniston Cold lost an eye. The action which took place in a field near Skipton station was known as the Anna Hills Fight, as a consequence of which six plug drawers were tried at York and imprisoned.

We are very fortunate to have on tape a conversation recorded many years ago, by a man whose father actually witnessed the rioters on their way to Skipton in 1842. The speaker was the late Mr John Robert Exley of Kelbrook, then an elderly gentleman and member of a most talented family. (He was still taking painting lessons in Skipton at the ege of 82).

'When my father were a little lad, there was a footpath down the meadow to the road—never used now—and a style at the bottom. My father was about 7 or 8 years old, when all t'rioters came towards Kelbrook. He had a cousin—a young fellow from Hague House working nearby. The rioters told him to join them, but his cousin said he had 'nowt to feight wi', so one o't'rioters pulled a brand new knife from his pocket, and said, 'Go to that sump 'oil and get a stick.' (The young man went to cut himself a stick from a bush growing around a boggy place, but wisely did not return!)

John Robert continues, 'They didn't bother my father, you see, because he were nobbut a lad. The rioters went on and drew t'plug at Dotcliffe (Kelbrook Mill). They were Plug Drawers—Chartists, they were called, weren't they? Anyway, a chap called Wasney—he's buried in Thornton Churchyard—must have heard that the rioters were coming from Burnley, and he met 'em on horseback somewhere about Kelbrook Church. They stopped him and said he would have to go with them, but he gave 'em a guinea to let them through, as he said he had important business to attend to.' (What they didn't know was that Wasney was actually on his way to Burnley to alert the Hussars!) 'Anyway, the rioters went on to Skipton.'

John Robert heard what happened at Skipton later from others who were there. 'They'd brocken into shops and getten owt they could—cheese, bread, owt they could rob, you know. Eventually the Horse Soldiers arrived in Skipton—they'd getten in a meadow somewhere—women an'all. They had to read the Riot Act three times and then they charged! T'women were running through t'quick thorn hedge to escape, and the soldiers hooked up their skirts with bayonets to let 'em go! That's what they telled my father, some as were there.'

What a fascinating description, recounted from an actual eye-witness account!

In spite of the strength of feeling at the time, there was no putting the clock back, and Dewhurst's business continued to grow. It had concentrated on cotton yarns and manufacturing cotton mixed goods, but in 1869 a major decision was taken, when it was decided to produce sewing cotton, leading eventually to Skipton becoming known as 'the home of Sylko'. By 1884 there were over 1000 employees, including office staff. In 1888 the family business was converted into a private company, John Dewhurst and Sons Ltd., and a little later, in 1897 the English Sewing Cotton Company was formed, comprising 14 firms, two of which, Dewhursts and Rickards were based in Skipton. Whatever the change of name, however, to Skiptonians the mill was always 'Dewhurst's'.

Toward the end of the 19th Century, cotton was being spun and woven at Belle Vue, and mercerised sewing cotton manufactured on a large scale, and dyed with a range of over 300 shades. The HQ of the firm was Arkwright House, Manchester, and in order to maintain high standards, weekly samples were sent from Belle Vue to Manchester, where there was a large Testing Department and Chemical Laboratory. By now, Sylko was widely distributed at home and overseas.

Mrs Dorothy Carthy records her experiences of working for the firm.

'In March 1939 I went to work at John Dewhurst & Co Ltd, part of the English Sewing Cotton Company in Skipton.

When vacancies at local firms occurred, they often rang the Girls' High School to see if they had any girls who were interested—I went for an interview and on entering the building was greeted by a commissionaire complete with gold braid, and eventually I was informed that the job was mine. I was the shorthand typist in the Thread Office, starting work at 7.45am and finishing at 5.30pm working on Saturday morning until mid-day, one hour for lunch and the wages were-£1 per week. Fares to Skipton had to be paid out of this, but the firm paid half which was very good as other firms paid no contribution to fares. I left home in Barnoldswick on the 6.50am bus and arrived back at 6.20pm almost a 12 hour day.

Secure jobs were important at this time and working at Dewhursts was considered to be a job for life. There were many departments in the Thread Section, which comprised the centre block of the mill buildings, the Spinning Department being nearest the houses on Broughton Road. On my first morning I was taken through the departments on my way to the Thread Department Manager's Office which was on the top floor across the corridor over Brewery Lane. I remember passing through the Polishing, Hand Spooling and Cop Section on the way. The Dyehouse was on the other side of the main road. A kind of gantry connected the buildings and letters could be sent over in a cylinder through a series of tubes housed in the Thread Office.

All workers including the office staff were supplied with two overalls with a different colour for each department. The office staff's were green and we each had a locker where we could hang our coats etc.

This was the period just before the outbreak of the Second World War which fewer and fewer people can remember. Most work people went home for dinner (now called lunch) and there was a great exodus from Dewhursts at 12.30. Those who travelled to work would eat their sandwiches in the 'Welfare' now part of the car park at Great Mills but most people in Skipton

Aerial view of Dewhurst's Mill.

went home. Walking up into Skipton at dinnertime on the Friday before the War was declared on Sunday I saw news placards outside the Cock and Bottle which read 'Germans bomb Warsaw' and we all wondered what was in store for us. The effect on Dewhursts was immediate, as the Spinning Department went on to overtime working, starting at 6am producing thread in khaki and blue for the Army and RAF. Conscripts came into Skipton and we could see them coming up the road from the Station and then doing their 'square-bashing' in the Auction Mart yard. Letters arrived saying SS Ship so-and-so had been sunk and the supply of wooden spools would not be arriving. Young men left to join the Forces and travelling in the black out was not easy, so when a job became available in Barnoldswick I left Dewhursts but still have happy memories of working there.' (Mrs Carthy later re-trained as a teacher).

During the Second War the firm had to demonstrate its versatility by switching to the manufacture of different yarns for the requirements of war—heavy yarns for haversacks or machine gun belts, and varying yarns from mosquito nets and bandages to flying suits, and many problems had to be overcome. Electric cabling, for instance, was covered with Dewhurst's polished yarn for purposes of insulation and to prevent wear, but in the jungles of the Far East this proved highly susceptible to attack form very un-English bacteria. It was discovered that the polish—a combination of starch, wax and soap, was providing a free meal-ticket to the jungle bugs, and a less attractive, nasty-tasting diet had to be devised, but one which would still do the job.

Dewhurst's provided life-long employment for some Skiptonians, the longest period of employment said to be that of Walter Whitaker who worked there for 62 years. Among other long-service awards was that of James Moorhouse who worked at the mill from 1887-1948 (61 years).

It seemed unthinkable that Dewhurst's which was so much a part of Skipton, would ever close down in the town, but in February 1983 the unthinkable happened, when the winding up of the operation was announced, and 240 jobs were lost. . . But Skipton adapted and survived. The substantial Belle Vue Mill is now premises for a company manufacturing Kingsley Cards. Plastic spools are produced in another section.

Other manufacturing concerns were established in the late 19th Century, among them Firth Shed which was built in 1877 by Samuel Farey. Here winceys and dyed cotton was made for the Bradford and Manchester trade. In 1926 the property was sold to Mark Nutter's from Nelson, concentrating on artificial silk, dress fabrics, umbrella cloths, curtains and quilts, and selling direct to the makers-up. A lot of workpeople accompanied Mark Nutter's from Nelson, and many were allocated council houses on the Burnside estate which had just been built. At Mark Nutter's there was cotton, silk, figured

Presentation at Mark Nutter's Mill.

corset material, and jacquard weaving, the jacquards putting the pattern in. Mark Nutter's also made vast quantities of parachute silk, and 1000 looms were operating on Firth Street. (Now, Merrit and Fryers, Builders) During the war, parachute silk was available without clothing coupons—probably spoilt pieces and so on. Anyway, underwear, blouses, and even wedding dresses were commonly made from this material, when parachutes had to be dismantled to make the garments.

Mr Fred Atkinson worked at Mark Nutter's, where it was his job to go round the mill collecting the 'pieces'. (finished lengths of cloth) He also ran a cutting machine to fold the cloth, which operated by a blade going back and forth. Fred's wife, Doreen, also worked in textiles as a weaver.

One un-nerving experience occured when 'something to do with the governors' went wrong and the mill engine 'ran away' sending the shafting round twice as quickly as normal while picking-sticks sent shuttles flying in all directions.

Around 1935-6 when Fred was 15 there was a disastrous long and bitter strike, occasioned by workers trying to insist on all-union labour. After many long weeks it failed, but relations at the mill were never quite the same again. Before the strike there had been a special train commissioned to take the workforce for a memorable day out to Blackpool, when the women were handed chocolates, the men cigarettes. After the strike this much looked-forward-to event seemed to 'fizzle out'. Rycrofts also had an annual day off at a different time, and they had been real treats for everyone.

Mrs Atkinson records her experiences as a weaver in the 1930s, when weaving was sometimes known as 'Poverty knocking'.

'In 1932 I was 14 years old, and in spite of my longing to be a trained hairdresser, I was put to the loom. My brother, however, had to have 'a trade in his fingers' so that he could one day keep a wife, and so he got an apprenticeship. Me, I was taken to Rycroft and Hartley's Mill in Broughton Road, Skipton. This entailed a two-mile walk across the fields from Carleton, to be at the mill by 7 o'clock every morning, except Sunday.

The first morning I entered the Looming and Twisting Room upstairs to be a 'reacher-in'—passing the long threads of twist from a beam, through the reeds to the 'loomer', who prepared the warp for the loom. The loomer was usually an old man of about 40! Sometimes he was quite 'ratty', and to make us jump to it he would dig his reed hook into our fingers as we passed him the thread.

After six weeks I was taken down to see the shed manager, who in those days seemed like 'God' to me. Archie took one look at me—"By, tha's nobbut a little 'un, ah'll 'ev to get thee a standin' board." This was 6 feet long, 4 inches deep, and about 3 feet wide, and raised me up to look over the shafts.

The noise was almost deafening, but over the years weavers became very skilful at lip reading and sign language. My teacher, Miss Macenearney was paid £3 in notes for teaching me this great skill. Although known as 'Poverty Knockers', weavers were really highly skilled workers.

I was taught to weave, even Jacquard material, beautifully embossed curtaining, the pattern picked out and woven in by turning a peg card, like the music that is played on a fairground organ; also umbrella cloth with a split in the middle, so that you were actually weaving two at once. Three months later, I was taken on to the 'rabbit run', a single line of looms, one for each of us trainee weavers.

We had such fun while training, not at all the image of 'dark Satanic mills'. In fact, when the Duke of Kent and Princess Marina were married, we found old warp ends for a wedding veil, and any old piece of satin to pin round us for wedding dresses, and we paraded up and down the run. When we got four looms after 12 months, we had really grown up. The work was hard, and £2 per week was an enormous wage at that time. Every year we had the Annual Ball at Christmas time, and the firm hired a complete train to take us all to Blackpool, including a ticket for lunch and admission to the Tower during the summer months. When Fred and I were married in 1940, he had to fill a huge green chamber pot (a wedding present) with beer for the men to have a drink for luck. I continued to weave until I was called up to the railway in 1941, when I became a lorry driver.'

Doreen signs herself 'A one-time happy Poverty Knocker'.

Mrs Atkinson penned in poetry form, her thoughts on the industry with which she has been associated all her life.

Changes through the ages

Sometimes I sit and think
Of how things used to be,
When our lovely ancient town
Was a hive of industry
Skipton—alias Sheeptown
For centuries
Your trade was in your name.
Came the hungry Thirties
When of course,
Changes came.
Weaving silks and satins,
Taffetas and umbrella cloths too,
Dewhursts' spinning Sylko thread

For all the world to sew.
1939. All change again.
This time its for war!
New skills swiftly learned in weaving,
Danger knocking on England's door.
Parachute silks, barrage balloon cloth,
Uniforms produced by the score,
Four looms, then six. . .
Sometimes a couple more.

. . . .

Gone now our manufacturing skills,
Silent our town
Now they've closed
All the mills.
No more the flying shuttle
Or bouncing cotton reel.
What next for Skipton
On the turn of fortune's wheel?

Some of the manufacturing concerns in Skipton were:—
Union Mills, Newtown—making ties, tablecloths, umbrella coverings;
Wilkinson's Mill, Brougham Street—a dyehouse mill, dyeing cops;
Rycroft and Hartley, Broughton Road—weaving;
Tosnay's Dyehouse, Walton Houses—occupied by Recket and Colman during War II;
Mark Nutter (Firth Street) Middletown—cotton and silk;
Moorhouses, (part of the Waterboard) bottom of Russell Street—cotton checks;
Sackville Mill—weaving textiles (Firth and Moorhouse) part of same block.

Quite often the manufacturers were self-made men who had worked hard and long to become established, and not all 'made it' successfully. Those who did and became employers, rose on the social scale and lived in residences befitting their status, but some never forgot the days when they themselves wore clogs on the factory floor. In the Broughton Road area, was a large imposing house, later a Children's Home, at one time referred to locally as 'Clog Hall' because the owner had reputedly 'risen from the ranks'. Another manufacturer in a nearby village regularly travelled First Class on the train from Skipton to Manchester—but always in his clogs, and on retirement he had a pair of clogs enshrined under a glass dome on the sideboard.

The men who maintained the machinery were the overlookers, colloquially known as 'tacklers', and they could make life pleasant or unpleasant for the weavers whose looms were in their charge. Perhaps as a way of retalliation, many 'tacklers' tales' circulated, slightly ridiculing these men, who for good or ill had so much influence on a weaver's life.

Typical are the following:—

'A tackler's wife was lying ill in bed, and the doctor instructed her husband, to give her a dose of powder sufficient to cover a sixpenny piece (small silver coin, known as a 'tanner', size of a new 5p piece.)

The next day the woman was very much worse.

"Did you give her the powder as I told you?" asked the doctor.

"Well," answered the tackler, "It were this way. I hadn't a tanner, so I gave her it on five pennies and two halfpennies!"

And what about this?

'Two tacklers decided to go camping in the country, but forgot to take pillows. Finding two drain pipes lying about, they used these as substitutes. In the morning one man complained of a stiff neck, and asked his mate how he had gone on.

"Oh, I've been all reight," said the other. "Tha sees, Tom, I stuffed mine wi' straw!"'

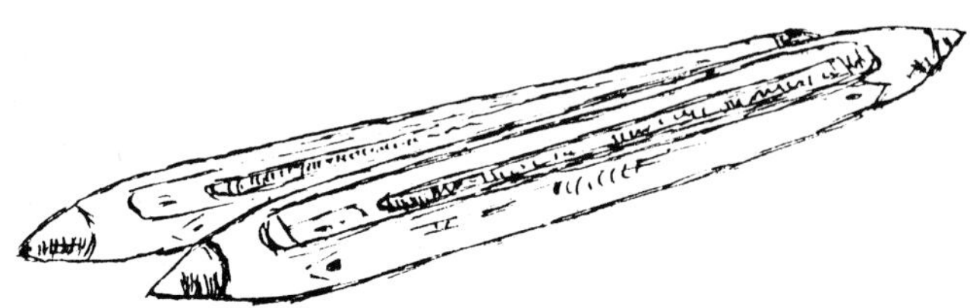

XII

How the town 'ticked' between the Wars — Shops and Businesses

BETWEEN the wars there were many more small shops and businesses, particularly family grocers, each with its own individual character—as supermarkets had not yet made their appearance. The Co-op movement, which had first become established in 1861, was now thriving, and there were small corner Co-ops in Gargrave Road, Broughton Road, Sackville Street and Keighley Road, and Duke Street, when divi-day was relied upon for that bit of spare cash that was often already 'spoken for'.

George E. Carr had numerous grocers' shops with their main premises on Sackville Street. The firm is remembered for its 'pink of perfection' boiled hams which were distributed all over the country. Other familiar names were Stockdale and Helms, Clideros, Walkers, Shuttleworths, Wades, David Jones, Harrisons and Pethybridges. Many orders were delivered within the hour—sometimes on a bike with a basket in front—and in fact customers were better served than they are today, since one never had very far to walk to the nearest grocer's anyway. (Supermarkets are fine, as long as you can see the prices and can drive a car). The outbreak of the 1939 war and introduction of rationing put paid to the delivery service generally.

An ex-customer recalls, 'Our family's weekly shopping was done at Harrison's Grocer's, situated on Keighley Road, where the car park now is, opposite the bottom of Castle Street. (Castle Street used to be open to Keighley Road, but had a fancy railing put across after a horse and cart once ran away, crossed the main road and ended up in Harrison's shop). The like of this quaint old-fashioned shop will never be seen again. There was a window on either side, and you went up a few steps into the middle of the shop, which always had a glorious smell of coffee and cheese and syrup and butter and currants all rolled into one, an aroma never encountered today, now that everything is packaged and de-humanised. There was a counter at either side, with a door into 't'back 'oil', and you had to peer through great slabs of butter on porcelain dishes, and brass weighing scales, and bags of this and that, in order to be served.

Dick and Mary Harrison ran their shop, ably assisted for years by white-

G. Sutherland, Middle Row. Ready for Christmas.

coated Herbert Bailey and Ivan Stratter who drove the van. Dick Harrison travelled from village to village once a month seeking orders, and following them up with his delivery van. Sometimes his travels took him about a week, and he went as far afield as Sedbergh, mostly by public transport. The grocery-books were like old passports, with hard backs and a little window for your name—far superior to anything on offer in this day and age. Dick was a real character, looking like something out of Dickens as he leaned over the counter looking over the top of his steel rimmed glasses. He would say in a confidential whisper, "Ah've just getten some fresh tins o'peaches (or pears or salmon, or whatever), Aye. . . They're reight grand 'uns, they are. (More confidentially) Are they owt in your line?" It usually worked.

As a small child I went into Harrison's shop one Saturday afternoon, when they were particularly busy. Mrs Harrison quickly stuffed handsful of uncounted pount notes into a paper bag, and asked me to nip up to the Bank in the High Street before closing time. I remember that the notes counted out to £80. Enough to buy half a house! And how trusting they were in those days. I suppose it never even occurred to her that I might have helped myself on the way.'

As I say, each grocer's had its own individuality. There was another shop up Newmarket Street where the cat could regularly be seen in the window, sitting on the cheeses!

Mrs Gladys Yeadon, who lived in Bright Street, remembers that there were more door-to-door hawkers at that time, and gipsies trying to sell lace and wanting to tell fortunes. 'There was also a number of people who came into the back street crying their wares. Mr Denny had a hand-cart on iron tyres, which was very noisy on the setts. He called out "Ice-cream," in summer, and "Hot peas," in winter, but if, in summer his sales were not going too well, his frustrated cry changed from "Ice-cream" to "ICE-CREE-AM!" Mr George Bradley came weekly from Bradley with horse and cart selling vegetables and fruit. His cry was, "Owt today? Owt today?" An old man appeared on Tuesdays in winter with shrimps, calling out "Morecambe shrimps!" and selling from a basket covered in a white cloth. He had two enamelled mugs as measures, the larger one was a shilling, the smaller, sixpence. Rag and bone men shuffled along with sacks calling out, "Any rags or bones? Any old iron?" Mrs Leach from Hardcastle's Yard (now,I think where the printing works is), came selling oat cakes, muffins and crumpets, which were, I think made in Hardcastle's Yard.' (Gladys watched these oat-cakes being made on a back-stone as late as the early thirties). Another familiar figure was 'Old Peg-Leg Wilson' who sold baskets, pegs, oilcloth and rugs.

Gladys continues, 'The stalls in the High Street on Saturdays made quite an animated scene on dark nights, after tea, when they were lit by naptha

Dobson's Chemists 1898.

flares. One vendor, outside Barclay's Bank sold drapery, but was such a comedien that people gathered round as much for the entertainment as to buy. All perishables were sold off cheaply after about 9 o'clock, there being no freezers, and some people habitually hung about until later to get their food at knock-down prices.'

At Ship Corner was Hopwood and Deakin's Sale Room, and Miss Windle had a millinery and drapery shop, while across Keighley Road, Simpson's were Mens' Outfitters, as were W.A. Simpson's in Swadford Street. Hurst's on Belmont Bridge catered for ladies' and mens' clothing, and other Ladies' Outfitters included Fort's in Sheep Street, and Boothman's haberdashery at the corner of Otley Street.

Towards the top end of High Street was Mrs Ambler's Ladies Outfitters, which after a few hiccups eventually became Rackham's. Mrs Ambler herself, was a somewhat formidable lady, who, if a customer was procrastinating, thought nothing of reminding her that it was time she made up her mind. Dresses and coats were upstairs, but downstairs she sold smaller items, including fully-fashioned pure silk stockings in the days before nylon became a household word . . . and if you had an account at Mrs Ambler's, well, you were well up the social ladder.

Mr Frank Watkinson had yet another Men's Outfitters in Caroline Square. His assistant was Mr Jowett, looking every inch a Field-Marshall with his straight back, immaculate clothes, and waxed moustache twisted up stiffly at the edges.

There were several family chemists, Green's, later Harry Brown's Frank Irving's in Sheep Stret, Illingworth's (now Hepper's), and Dobson's next door to Whittaker's.

Clogs were often worn. (Popular with children and weavers because they lifted the feet up from the cold concrete floor of the mills). There were several clogger's shops, including two Clogger Thompsons, Mr Bank's Cloggery, and Meakin's on Keighley Road. Since horses had not then been entirely replaced by motorised vehicles, there were also various blacksmiths, including Wards at the bottom of Raikes and one over Belmont Bridge, by the canal.

Waterfall's Book Shop, (with its famed minstrel's gallery), was up the High Street and the Craven Herald shop and offices were in their present position. There were numerous sweets and tobacconists's shops dotted about the town, including Overend's on Swadford Street.

M.E.L. recalls, 'I have reason to remember Overend's shop, because every Saturday it was my appointed task to travel on the 'Silver Star' bus from Bradley, more or less specially to buy an ounce of smoking twist for my father. Mr Overend was a tall, refined gentleman, who always seemed to be discussing important issues of the day with his customers. Anyway, this 'twist' was

Thomas Boothman's family butcher, Sheep Street.

always wrapped up in brown paper, twirled round at one end, and I called for this weekly, quite happily, until one day I happened to read in the newspaper that it was illegal for children under a certain age to buy tobacco. This included me, and the following Saturday, for the first time, my heart was in my boots as I set off on my usual mission, there being no escape. Mr Overend served me as usual, and I popped the tobacco in its twirl of brown paper into the bottom of an otherwise empty basket. Heaving a sigh of relief that I had not been arrested for this heinous crime, I proceeded along Swadford Street, when to my horror, out of the corner of my eye, I spied a police car drawing up at the kerb, right alongside me! There was no doubt in my mind but that retribution was at hand, and in my panic I started to run. Of course, I tripped on a flagstone and fell full length, the basket flew out of my hand, and the twist spilled out on the pavement. By this time the policeman was close behind. My heart nearly stopped as he gently took my arm to pick me up, and nonchalently retrieving the twist from the pavement, he popped it safely back into my basket! As far as I was concerned he could have been handling a stick of dynamite! How was I to know that he was only on his way to post a letter at the post office further down!

During this period there were many small butcher's shops in and around the town. German pork butchers were well established in Craven, including Schultz, at one time in the Middle Row. It is said that the butcher used to walk through the streets with his sleeves rolled up, stirring a bucket of blood to prevent it from curdling.

Mr Norman Dexter was a barber and haircutter, who served his time with Fred Cork of Sheep Street, until he set up business on his own account. He believed that Corks had been cutting hair in various premises in the town for over two hundred years. The day started at 8.30am, closing down at 8 o'clock each night, but later on Fridays and Saturdays, and with one hour off for dinner. Wages were 8 shillings a week, rising by 2 shillings each year of the 7-year apprenticeship. Downstairs there was a room for the so-called working class, with a room upstairs for those prepared to pay more. 'Better off' customers had their own pot and shaving brush which was left at the shop. Men's hair was cut regularly every 2-4 weeks when the fashion was 'short back and sides', and work was made easier when the first electric clippers came in, about 1930. Some customers went into the shop for the companionship as much as a haircut and kept a weather eye open for Frank Whalley or Arthur Pethybridge, when there was likely to be much leg-pulling. Sometimes, for instance, when there were four or five people in front of him, a client would tire of waiting and dash off, prompting the comment, "It's a bit of a beggar when a bloke comes in and reads all t'books and then beggars off!" At other times, among the banter, the proprietor would be accused of making a profit

Thomas Cork's shop, Sheep Street 1898.

out of the hair cut off.

It is impossible to mention every business that made the town tick, but there was always someone to fulfil a need. Hutchinsons had a Rolls Royce hearse, driven at funerals by Charlie Mathers for many years. Baldwins had horse-drawn conveyances and Woodwards had horses kept in stables at the back of the Devonshire hotel. The same horses were also required to pull the fire engine, and it is said that if a fire broke out on the odd occasion when a funeral was in progress, the horses would be diverted from the cortege to go to the fire. Woodwards also had a horse-drawn fever-cart, which would transport the patient to the Fever Hospital, blinds drawn, like the harbinger of doom it so often was.

It is a fact that many infectious diseases such as scarlet fever and diptheria posed a real threat and cost many young lives. Tuberculosis was another killer, but happily this threat has been largely removed, although other even more lethal diseases such as Aids, are already taking their places.

The age of motorised transport was gaining a foothold in the early part of the century. George Bishop was a motor engineer and he and Elijah Raw built the first motor car in Skipton in the old Fire Station. This they tried out on Water Street. Bicycles were also made there by the firm of Bishop-Scheroot, the Scheroot half of the partnership being Dutch.

Ledgard and Wynn is a prestigious name in Skipton, selling beautiful furniture and china. Earlier, Wynns had a pawnbroking business in Newmarket Street. Another firm that went from strength to strength was that of Mr Tom Clarke, who after the war opened premises on Coach Street, where he brought in flock matresses for teasing and cleaning. There had to be something better to sleep on, and Tom's business developed into a thriving nation-wide concern, 'Silentnight' spring matresses, now with large premises at Barnoldswick, Salterforth and Sutton.

Oltey Street is one of the Skipton's best-known streets, branching off, as it does, from the tree-lined High Street. Mrs Doreen Atkinson remembers it as it was from about 1940 until after the war.

'In 1940 the traffic could go both up and down this narrow street, which had a variety of shops and offices.' To name but a few:—

'Miss Leach, tailoress and dressmaker here had her shop, displaying perhaps just one exquisitely tailored suit or 'costume'. She was a large lady, always elegantly dressed, wearing ear rings and long strings of beads about her person.' (Barbara Mason remembered that Miss Leach lived in a delightful cottage in one of the yards, with a padded red leather seat along the wall, and upstairs, little steps going over a beam. Barbara was once given a tiny kettle by Miss Leach for adding whisky or gin to tea.) Nearby was Miss Cairns, Corsetier, for in those days many women still wore lace-up corsets, stiffened with whalebone. Mrs Atkinson continues, 'The entrance to Bank Yard was well set back from the road, through an archway which led to a delightful cobbled yard fronting seven very old cottages, each with a tiny garden set in the egg-shaped cobbles, with roses and ivy climbing up the old stone walls. Outside privies were at each end, and a flight of stone steps led to Thompson's Painters and Plumbers Warehouse.'

As industry developed, and the population increased, so whole new areas sprang up to accommodate the workers. Middletown was one such district. E.W. writes:—

'In the Twenties Middletown housed a close-knit community of hard working people who followed a wide range of employment. This area was often classed as a rough quarter, but this designation was quite unjustified. These citizens were 'tough and ready' rather than 'rough and ready'. To their own community they were caring and considerate people, good neighbours who reponded instantly to any appeals for help from the poor and needy (and there were plenty of those). At the same time they steadfastly retained their individualism and pride.

At this time there was a clan-like tendency to classify other residents of Skipton according to the area in which they lived. 'Newtowners', 'Spring Gardeners', 'Broughton Roaders' and 'Gargrave Roaders' were the 'tags' used, yet when the Whitsuntide walks or the Gala Day parades took place, everyone willingly responded, displaying their collective pride in being 'Skiptonians'.

Sackville Street was the hub of Middletown and supplied a number of commodities via many small family businesses. The streets that radiated towards Castle Street had a shop at each corner, and within easy reach were cloggers, drapery stores, sub-post-office, greengrocers, grocers, fish and chip shop, confectioners, ice-cream and pie and pea outlet, off-licence, butchers, newsagent, chemist and herbalist, seedsman and florist, jeweller and clock repairer, printers and stationers, fent shop, joiners and undertakers, builders and stonemasons and general stores selling dolly-blues, scouring stones, red carbolic roap, yeast and all home baking requirements.

E.W. describes Romille Street, where Butterfield's Barbers Shop and Newsagent was situated. 'Here I spent many happy hours as a newspaper boy and lather-boy' Nearby was the Temperance Hall which had a large room available for concerts, dances and meetings, and provided Bed and Breakfast accommodation for tourists and travellers.

'Further entertainment was provided by the building next door, the Gem Picture House. There one enjoyed the daring exploit of Pearl White and Ruth Rowland, the villainies of Eric von Stroheim and Warner Oland in 'Fu Manchu'. William S. Hart and Tom Mix satisfied the 'cowboys' amongst us, and comedy was provided by the antics of Larry Semon and Chester Conklin. To enjoy the galaxy of these delights, we paid 'thrupence' for the privilege of occupying a formlike wooden seat at the front of the cinema.'

Nearing Keighley Road, there were shops on the ground floor of an imposing building, known as the Liberal Club Buildings. The first floor encompassed an up-to-date Assembly Room of generous proportions, a Billiard and Snooker Room. Lecture, Reading and Smoking Rooms were available. One could even have a bath here!

Small boys would sometimes have recourse to Bower's Yard, for here was the shop and works of Mr Tindall, Metal Worker and Cycle Repairer, who mended the broken iron hoops on the 'bogies' that children constructed from old pram wheels fixed to boards.

'Brougham Street Council School catered for the educational requirements of the district, under the guidance of Mr Townsend, the headmaster, who provided so much for his pupils.

Really, Middletown was a self-contained village within a town, whose inhabitants reacted to that environment of isolation. Yet they enjoyed occasional 'forays' to the larger town of skipton, but always felt more comfortable in their own territory.'

Broughton Road was another district with its own character, housing many rail workers. Belle Vue Mills was one of the landmarks in this area, and to a lesser degree 'Owd Bill's Garage' run for many years by Mr Bill Wiseman. According to one ex-Broughton Roader, early in the war there was a serious fire at 'Owd Bill's', when the heat was so intense that the silver melted in the till. A Great Dane emerged from the flames with its coat on fire, but when the firemen turned their hoses on it, it ran off, and did not reappear for some days, when it had recovered from its ordeal.

Premises of Mr Thomas Fattorini, Caroline square 1898.

XIII
Thomas Fattorini (Skipton) Ltd

'FATTORINI' is a name synonymous with Skipton, and rolls off the Skiptonian's tongue as easily as Brown, Smith or Hartley. Fattorini's have been associated with the town for so long that it would be hard to envisage Skipton without this well-known and respected family.

Fattorini's outlined their firm's history in a leaflet published in 1967 to mark 140 years of continuous service. It was in 1815, during the reign of George IV, that there was a real threat of invasion of England by Napoleon, happily resolved for us by a British victory at Waterloo. The statesmen at that time seemed to be unusually far-seeing. In order to win the peace, they decided to introduce new industries and develop trade by encouraging other Europeans to settle here who had crafts at their fingertips, not then widely practised in this country. So it was that the founders of the firm of Fattorini's accepted the government's invitation, and brought to England their aptitude in watchmaking skills and knowledge of the jewellery trade.

Having settled in Skipton, the 'Gateway to the Dales', they soon realised the potential of supplying barometers to Dales farming communities, whose lives were inextricably bound up with weather conditions, particularly in hay and harvest times. Mr Fattorini made business trips to various parts of the Dales on horseback about every three months, and it says much for mutual trust, in that a barometer would be left on approval and without obligation until the next business trip into that area. Dales farmers, having practised frugality in order to survive, had an innate scepticism towards 'new-fangled' innovations, but it is recorded that after testing, not one single instrument was ever returned.

Mr Wilfred Fattorini records, 'Thomas Fattorini', my father, whose name was adopted by the firm, was born in Skipton and lived in New Street, Skipton (now Otley Street), As a child, he went to a local little Dame School run by the Misses Kipling, aunts to Rudyard Kipling. '(The Revd Joseph Kipling was a Methodist minister living in Otley Street. He and his wife are buried in the Old Cemetery up Raikes Road.)' In 1863, his father-in-law built the corner premises of Caroline Square/Newmarket Street and the firm operated from there until the move to Carleton in 1936/7. The firm has always had a Birmingham connection and today makes every kind of badge and civic insignia.

In fact the City of Westminster Lord Mayor's Badge of Office was made by us.'

The business developed and was conducted as a high class country jewellers, with trade largely at the counter. Further, by 1874, Mr Fattorini was inviting appro. parcel requests, which he undertook to dispatch the day the order was received. Additional building work later took place, but in spite of this the Skipton premises became too small for the expanding mail-order business, which prompted the firm to move to more commodious mill premises at nearby Carleton in 1937. Two years later, however, the Second World War broke out, with disastrous consquences. Anyone who has not lived during a World War does not realise the extent to which it took over every aspect of our lives. Living in wartime was living under a virtual dictatorship—everything had to be sublimated to winning the war—and firms or individuals had to do as they were told, with no arguing, or else... Accordingly in 1941, at half past five one Friday afternoon, Fattorini's received notice that their Carleton premises were to be requisitioned for war purposes, and arrangements had to be made, almost at a moment's notice, to disperse the staff of some 350 employees. Indeed, at 9am the following morning there was a token occupation of the building by the Ministry of War's nominees. This was a shattering blow to a firm which had been established in the district for a hundred years, and there was to be no compensation. Fortunately, a small office had been kept ticking over in Caroline Square, and it was here that Fattorini's kept a nominal firm in existence.

Many Skiptonians and girls from surrounding villages found employment at Fattorini's between the wars, among them Elsie Easterby, formerly Elsie Milne, who started work at the Caroline Square premises in the 1920s. Elsie has very happy memories of the years she spent with the firm, which she describes as 'very good to work for'. At that time three large windows opened on to Caroline Square. Rows and rows of office workers dispatched orders, and upstairs there was a packing department, with floors specially strengthened to accommodate the safes. In those days there were many competitive sporting events, and Fattorini's supplied sports trophies, medals and cups, which were ordered from Birmingham.

Mr Arrigoni was in charge of the retail section, where a person was employed specifically for cleaning the silver. Decorum was the order of the day, and girls on the retail side were expected to wear black or navy blue dresses, or dark overalls.

It is of interest that early in the century many smart wedding receptions were held at the Devonshire Hotel opposite. Fattorini's provided a valuable service in that wedding presents would be sent across to the firm's premises, where they would be tastefully displayed in a special room with good security arrangements. Later, they would be packed and directed to the newly-weds' home.

Perhaps the secret of the Fattorini's success was, that although dealing in high-class luxury goods, they never lost the 'common touch'. Elsie recalls how occasionally, Dales country people—working farmers and so on—would come into the shop, to have, say, a watch or clock repaired. If Mr Fattorini was aware of this, he would immediately take them into his private office, and Elsie would be sent across to Hartley's tea-shop in the Middle Row for a tray of tea and cakes. This was because during the years when Mr Fattorini had travelled the Dales seeking orders, he had often been at the receiving end of Dales hospitality, and as the firm prospered, he did not forget those who had helped it on its way.

Parish Church from Primrose Hill—early 20th Century.

XIV
Living Conditions—Early 20th Century

THERE have been tremendous strides in living conditions since the early 20th Century, but to those living at the time, change did not seem to come quickly. In the Daily Chronicle of 1926 (Jan 18th), Skipton was described, perhaps a little too graphically, as having the world's worst slums—houses where sun and air never reached. Specially mentioned were Union Square, (now demolished) by the canal over Belmont Bride, Chancery Lane, Club Houses and Canal Yard. Nevertheless, this was the England for which so many had given their lives in the First World War.

M.E.L. recalls, 'People from surrounding villages thronged to Skipton by bus on Saturday afternoons to do the weekly shopping. One of my first memories in the mid-Twenties, is pulling on my mother's hand, so that I could take a backward, curious glance at the legless men who were sitting on the pavement along Sheep Street and High Street. Beside them they had placed their upturned caps, into which shoppers would throw the odd coin as they passed. The lower part of these men's bodies was encased in a leather cushion. There were no wheel chairs for these unfortunates, but they propelled themselves along by holding in each hand a wooden half-roller, with a handle like a flat iron. They 'walked' by moving both rollered hands together on the stone pavement, and they then swung their bodies forward inbetween. Mr Arthur Brewer remembers once going into the men's lavatory at the King's Head, which was dimly lit by gas-light. He thought he was alone, and it was not until he heard a sneeze from the floor that he realised that there was a legless man in the shadows. As a child I remember accepting that some men didn't have legs as a fact of life, and it was not until many years later that I realised that they were, in fact, ex-servicemen from the 1914 War—heroes who had lost limbs in France, but were still condemned to a begging life at pavement level.'

On Saturday afternoons Skipton was full of life and bustle. Sometimes a kilted Scotsman would perform with his one-man band. Drum on his back, symbols between his knees, and bag-pipes in his hands, he would make music outside the Brick Hall. Or there would be a barrel organ or 'tingalarey' wheezing away complete with real, live monkey, and often a scissors-grinder would appear, pushing his outfit along on one wheel, until he turned it upside

Early 20th Century view of Grassington Road.

down and set it up ready for business. And where are the 'sandwich men'now, who mingled with shoppers encased back and front in boards? Nor would it have seemed like Saturday without the 'Sally Army's' hymn-singing and musical accompaniment at the end of Sheep Street. About 1925, a Russian with a dancing bear would attract a crowd on the setts near the Old George, and a fox in a wire cage was regularly on display outside the Little Ship, down the slope. The Little Ship Inn, (now offices) towards Mill Bridge had a bit of land at the back, but no path up the side, and it was not unusual for pigs to be run through the pub to loaden up!

The Coffee Tavern, almost opposite the end of Sheep Street, was a favourite meeting-place. This was lit by gas-light, and indeed the gas-light in the streets emanated from those picturesque Victorian lamp-posts, now so much sought after. The lamplighters would come round on edge of dark, carrying long poles with a flame at the end. Men worked in pairs, one doing the front, and one the back, of each street. He hooked his pole on to a chain to turn the gas on, and it was hooked to a chain at the other side, to turn the gas off, on the see-saw principle. A later innovation was a clock on a spring, set to come on at a certain time.

Mr Arthur Brewer, born 1917, lived in Russell Street, Middletown, which then had an unmade road, and well he remembers conditions at the time. His father worked in the quarry, his mother at Dewhurst's Mill, for it has long been a tradition, even a necessity, in this area for married women to go out to work, somehow rearing a family 'in and among'. Money was always tight. Mrs Brewer worked from 6am until 5.30pm and until 12.30 on Saturday mornings, earning 25 shillings a week. (£1.25) She baked on Saturday and washed on Sunday. The water was heated in a boiler by the fire, and there was no means of drying clothes in bad weather, except round the fireside.

A lot of household activities took place round the coal fire, the grate having to be cleaned out each morning, first job, with a cowl rake. Iron kettles and pans were 'boiled' on the open fire, (blocking most of the heat), and a hook hung down the chimney for frying bacon. Flat irons stood at the front, and were heated alternately on the glowing embers when required. Mr Brewer recalls that 'the mantlepiece was about six feet high', and the oven and boiler, besides having sooty flues to clean, also had to be blackleaded about once a week.

The stone-flagged floor was laid on a bed of ashes, which combined with the dampness, made an ideal environment for black-clocks. (Not to be confused with cockroaches). Periodically, Mrs Brewer got down on her hands and knees to scrub the stone floor. However, a pegged rug, made from scraps of old clothing, was rolled out at the week-ends in front of the fire, and duly rolled up again on Sunday nights when the flags once again had to suffice.

The luxury of linoleum came later.

The favourite foods were oven-bottom cake, rabbit stew, or a dish of potatoes, dripping and salt, and sometimes a sheep's head or oxtail which was bought cheaply from the stalls on a Saturday night. Now and again, a pudding would be made with threepenceworth of skimmed milk. Santa Claus DID visit the children at Christmas, to the tune of a Christmas stocking with an orange, apple, nuts, and a cracker to pull. At that time the property was owned by a private landlord (Harry Hague) and tenants were given a quarter of tea at Christmas. Another bonus was when Arthur's mother would bring home a large bag of wooden cotton reels from Dewhurst's. Some were used for kindling, but from others the children used to make their toys. Forget your modern battery-operated gadgets—it was wonderful what could be done with a penknife and a few elastic bands. A few nicks and twists, and a bobbin would move forward on its own, like a tank.

New clothes were bought for the Walking Round at Whitsuntide, and were afterwards worn for Sunday School, but had to be changed once children were back in the house. Old clothes were worn for school, patch upon patch and socks well darned, and after that handed down to the younger element whenever possible. The wardrobe was a nail behind the bedroom door. One poor family had many children, but not enough clothes to go round, and arranged matters so that half the children went to school in the mornings, but the other half attended in the afternoons, wearing the same clothes.

Clogs were the standard form of footwear in the Brewer household. They cost 4½d to be 'rung', (irons replaced), but sometimes even this was beyond the family's means. A complete 'clogging' operation (replacing wooden soles on to the leather uppers), cost all of 5 shillings, and sometimes more, if the thicker, 'donkey rings' were used. In time the leather uppers became almost too weak to stand the strain of another clogging (rather like new wine in old bottles), and this gave rise to an interesting expression. If a person, recovering from illness was asked how he was, he might reply, "Fair to middling. I shall clog again with a light sole!"

In spite of the general shortage of cash, 'Sunday' clothes generally were formal, and a young man was not considered to be 'dressed up' unless attired in a full suit with waistcoat. Boys never wore long pants until the age of about 15, when they appeared in long trousers, signalling to the world that they had grown up. Of course, fashions came and went, from knee-breeches to plus-fours, trilbies, spats and goloshers. Women and girls were enslaved to the current fashionable hem-line, frantically letting hems down or taking them up, so that they were the requisite number of inches below knee-length. Females also went through the whole gambit of whalebone corsets, lisle stockings, chemises, liberty bodices, fleecy elasticated bloomers (passion killers), and combinations (coms), probably the most unhygienic garment ever invented. Who now remembers fancy garters? These were about an inch wide, covered in ruched silk, usually in bright green, yellow or pink, decorated with rose-buds, and often worn provocatively just below the knee by otherwise staid middle-aged ladies.

The backyard was the location of the outside privy in Russell Street, and had a long wooden seat, with a bowl underneath into which buckets of water had to be poured manually, the contents then disappearing into the mains. Some houses had 'tippler' lavatories, also flushed manually. On a nail in the back-yard hung the family's tin bath. It was brought indoors on Friday nights when children were bathed in front of the fire—adults hardly ever.

Illness was an added nightmare in those days before the National Health service, because a visit to the doctor's was usually followed by a bill (except when the doctor 'forgot'). Consequently, much store was set by home remedies. To keep colds away you were dosed with cod-liver oil. Brimstone and treacle purified the blood, and bread poultices and Bates' Salve drew out matter from the boils which everyone seemed to have on the backs of their necks like miniature volcanoes. An old woman herbalist supplied cheap remedies such as marshmallow ointment or buttercup syrup, but there were times, of course, when the doctor had to be summoned. The Fishers are a long-established family of Skipton doctors, Doctors Robinson, MacLeod, Morrison, Liversidge, Barlow, Merlin and Goodall being other names associated with that era. In the early days doctors usually had a chauffeur, dressed appropriately in dark suit and peaked hat, who propelled the doctor about from patient to patient. (After all, we were still only a few steps away from the 'horseless carriage' and motor cars were few and far between).

As it happened, in those hard times, there was usually a ministering angel—someone to whom the community looked in times of trouble or distress. In Russell Street, this 'someone' was Mrs Barrett, a woman with enough cares of her own, but who always managed to give a hand where need be. It was Mrs Barrett who brought you into the world when you were born, and laid you out when you were dead. She would keep the household ticking over if a mother was laid up with a new baby, or do that extra bit of nursing, baking, or cleaning, if someone was ill. "I can see her now, as if it were yesterday," said Mr Brewer, "Standing there in her clogs and her red shawl." Mrs Barrett had seven children of her own—six sons and one daughter, all of whom predeceased her, except one, for in spite of her hard, sad life, she lived to be 96.

It seems that as our material prospects have improved, so our caring and consideration for others, has declined. In the Twenties, if the milk stood too long on the doorstep in Middletown, somebody would knock to see if you

Mrs Barrett's 'likeness'. (Her words).
She was an invaluable member of the community.

were all right—and you could go out all day leaving the door unlocked without fear of thieves taking advantage during your absence.

Pawn shops fulfilled a need in the deprivation of the day, and there were at least two pawn shops, one down Spencer's Yard, run by Mr Challenger, and Wynn's in Newmarket Street. People would take their wedding rings in on Mondays to be redeemed on Fridays, or would pawn suits of clothes, and the buskers who operated after the 1914 War would pawn their musical instruments for a bit of ready money. The buskers stayed at the Model Lodging House at the bottom of Commercial Street, or the Model at the top of Newmarket Street. Mr Brewer recalled that there were stalls up the Street on Mondays, Wednesdays, Fridays and Saturdays, which had to be removed each day by midnight and 'shoved into the pub yards'. Horses and carts had to be 'garaged' in Jerry Croft, where there were tying places and areas designated for depositing rubbish. .

Of course, similar conditions to the ones described, prevailed all over the industrial North. Mr Percy Ogden was headmaster of Ings School, Skipton, from 1941-1945. Born in 1901, he was brought up in Haworth, famed for its Bronte associations. As a boy, he trundled sandstone from the moor in a wheelbarrow, which he and his sisters then chopped up in the cellar. When reduced to sand this was scattered on the stone-flagged floors of the house, and clogged feet ground it up further. A lading-canful brought the colour up, and the sand absorbed spills and stains. The sand was swept up at weekends, when 'You couldn't see across the floor for dust.' The luxury of a roll of matting was then enjoyed, to be rolled up again at the start of the working week.

Spartan as times were, nevertheless, they had improved from Percy's grandfather's generation, for he was a hand-loom weaver who would regularly walk the 10 miles to Hebden Bridge, carrying a heavy finished 'piece' on his back, and returning with a sack of oatmeal to feed his family.

There were nine living children in Mr Ogden's family, and his mother made her boys' trousers from warp-ends from the mill, which were so stiff that their tiny fingers could hardly manipulate the buttons. For this reason, boys wore skirts until they could look after themselves. The children started school when they were three years old. Mr Ogden felt that he and his other brothers and sisters owed a debt of gratitude to their eldest sister, who could easily have pursued an academic career, but who had to leave school and work at the mill in order to pave the way for the rest. All the children of that family won scholarships to the Grammar School, seven becoming teachers, and one a chemist.

Parents had to make great sacrifices in those days to educate their children, which were appreciated because the privilege was hard-won. So often, in present times, children do not seem to value their opportunities, perhaps because they have been handed too much 'on a plate'.

Model Lodging House, bottom of Lower Commercial Street, demolished.

XV
The old order changeth

BEFORE the family car came into its own, there were excellent bus services, connecting up with almost anywhere in the country. Between the wars, buses ran from Caroline Square, including the Silver Star Motor Bus Co. to Bradley and Carleton, Laycock's to Barnoldswick, and the West Yorkshire Road Car Co. which started running circa 1928 to Keighley and Bradford. Pennine Buses to Gargrave and Settle started outside the Yorkshire Penny Bank.

Few tramps are now seen, but before the Second War it was a common sight to see gentlemen of the road tramping from one workhouse to another. The Union Workhouse up Gargrave Road (now Raikeswood Hospital) built in 1840, replaced the 'Poorhouse' down Broughton Road, but the present buildings were then obscured from prying eyes by a somewhat forbidding gatehouse. The Workhouse had basically two main functions. It granted food and loging to itinerant tramps, and it provided a roof for those elderly or incapacitated members of society who had nowhere else to go, bearing in mind that until 1909 there were no old age pensions. Elderly people of the Thirties used to tell how *their* parents and grandparents had to save every penny that could be spared during their working lives, in order to avoid 'ending up in the Workhouse'. A number of cripples lived there, and at one time there must have been many children for in 1871 it is recorded that 49 children from Skipton Workhouse went on a day trip to Morecambe. In its early days, conditions at the Workhouse were purposely kept Spartan by way of discouragement. At one time, for instance, couples were separated from each other until the age of 60 when they were allowed to sleep together.

Mr and Mrs Alfred Walker were in charge of the Workhouse for many years before its change of role. The Master, Mr Walker was treated with respect, and expected to be addressed as 'sir'. Between the wars there were still many able-bodied tramps who did a day's work in return for food and lodging, before being required to tramp on to either Keighley or Giggleswick. In a long, low, building, now pulled down, they broke up stone into pieces small enough to push through a mesh. The ground sloped down at the back, so that the stone could easily be shovelled up for use on roads and railways. It is said that not all tramps were as poor as they looked, and sometimes would hide their valuables in Botheby Wood before entering the gates.

Raikeswood Hospital (formerly the Workhouse) as it is today.

The regular 'inmates' of the Workhouse, before the Second War, wore uniforms—grey trousers and jackets made by Simpson's tailors. One rather bizarre feature was that in one of the buildings various sizes of coffins were stacked up at the ready!

The Workhouse was partially self-supporting, as pigs and hens were kept there, and vegetables grown. Some unemployed youths also did 'Test Work' there, and would be set to work sawing wood, being paid in vouchers in exchange for groceries, so as not to fritter away their earnings.

Mr Brewer's father worked at Skipton Rock, working until 8pm in summer, and five o'clock in winter. When a man started at the quarry, he worked three days 'for nowt', and overtime and Sunday work was paid at the same rate. The manager was Mr Hargreaves who later opened a quarry at Halton East. The workers took their own cold tea and sandwiches as there were no vacuum flasks. Only those of this vintage will appreciate the boon that plastic bags have brought, for in these pre-war days there was no means of preventing bread from going dry. If, in bad weather, workers were 'snown off' they would be sent instead snow-shifting, paid for by the railway or council. The stone from Skipton Rock, being shaly and not the quality of Bradley stone, mostly went to railways or roads for ballast, chippings, concrete floors, or between sleepers. The quarry had two steam engines, one for delivery to Embsay station, and the other went to the Woods to supply the Canal Company. The last 200 yards or so down to the canal was on an endless rope, manworked with a drum brake and handle. Two full wagons went down and dragged two empty ones up. The stone slid down a chute into the waiting boats, and once, when the wire broke, the tub accelerated too much and sank the boat. What a calamity! Skipton Rock is still operational, as is Skibeden Quarry up the Bailey. 'Joe Smith's Quarry', further up, was taken over by Tilcon, and another quarry up Moor Road, which made jambs, causeway kerbs and setts, is now closed.

Another big, and regrettable change, is the decline in moral standards. Children between the wars, had in some ways, more freedom than the present generation, which is loadened with material goods but faces hazards even when coming from school. Children in the Twenties and Thirties, spent hundreds of hours innocently roaming the countryside, with no real threat of being abducted, molested or assaulted. Though not angels, a code of right and wrong was instilled into the child at an early age, through Sunday School, or through moral teaching in Day School. To many families, public houses were taboo, for pubs were then mainly drinking places. (It has to be admitted that addiction to drink caused misery in some families, which is why you either went into pubs, or you stayed out completely). Drugs were not then a threat, and AIDS was a nightmare of the future. There were far fewer broken homes

Rear of Skipton Castle. Boats on Springs Canal loading stone from the quarry.

with divorces bringing countless problems in their wake.

It is much more difficult for caring parents to bring children up today, competing as they are with the violence and sex introduced into their own homes via television and represented as the norm. Between the wars, teachers, lecturers, and those in authority were expected to be on the side of the parents (publically, at least!) but now, so many are more concerned with their own trendy image. It is difficult for parents to try to uphold standards when engulfed in a sea of permissiveness, and when, to their offspring, they must often seem to be the only ones out of step.

Devonshire House, Albert Street (formerly Spencer's Yard) a handsome Georgian building demolished 1956 in spite of protest.

XVI
Recreation and Entertainment — Early 20th Century

IN THE early part of the 20th Century there was no television, but most people had a 'wireless set'. At first ear-phones were used, and the sound emenated from a large trumpet on the lines of 'His Master's Voice', but by the Second War battery-operated sets were in use, the heavy batteries, (with one in reserve), having to be regularly recharged. Television arrived after the war, but took some time to reach its present level of refinement. Around 1950, a local electrician caused a sensation when he rigged up a makeshift set in a wooden hut, and the invited inlookers gaped in wonder as shadowy figures flicked across the screen.

Nevertheless, there was plenty of entertainment of a different kind, even if it required some sort of effort. About every two years there were aeroplane flights from Ings Big Meadow. It cost 5 shillings to fly in a single-engined plane, sometimes piloted by Mr Fielding, whose father's shop, Fieldings' Mens' Outfitters, was in Swadford Street, next to Porri's China Shop. (They do say that if you remember Porri's you are getting a bit long in the tooth!). Another pilot was Skiptonian, W. Bateman. Sometimes the celebrated air ace, Alan Cobham himself, accompanied the flying entourage.

In 1909 the Olympic Roller Skating Rink was opened between Carleton New Road and the Leeds and Liverpool Canal—now part of a sawmill. This comprised some 7,500 square feet, with bandstand, promenade and refreshment bar. There were three sessions per day, morning admission 3d, with 6d for hire of skates. In the early days skates moved around to the soothing strains of an orchestra, but later an automatic organ was installed. The 1914-18 War, however, sounded the death knell of this enterprise.

Travelling menageries on the same site made periodic visits to Skipton, as did Buffalo Bill's Wild West Show, and there are frequent references in school log books to children absenting themselves to attend.

Many of the older generation will remember with nostalgia the Whitsuntide and Bank Holiday events, when Shaw's Fun Fair set up in the cattle market, Jerry Croft. Besides the usual roundabouts and swings and the odd helter-skelter, there were the inevitable boxing-booths, when gloves would

Coach leaving for Blackpool, at 5 shillings per head.

be thrown out as a challenge to the farm lads gathered around, who were promised their money back and a few coppers if they survived three rounds with a professional. A little man appeared every year inviting the macho youths of the day to test their strength by striking with a sledgehammer and hopefully ringing the bell at the top of the pole. In addition there were usually a few peep-shows, when payment was made to view some unfortunate person, grossly deformed, a two-headed calf or a five-legged foal—mutations which could not then be blamed on nuclear power. For some people these events would never have been the same without the little man who always turned up with small round potatoes, fried on the field.

M.E.L. remembers, 'As a child, once when in Skipton, I happened across an acquaintance from Bradley and we decided to visit the fair in Jerry Croft. I hadn't any money, but she had a whole penny which she decided to blue in, in one reckless throw. There were, at that time, certain stalls having a counter marked out in squares. You shot your coin from a little brass shovel, and if it fell clear of a line you claimed the amount marked on the square, usually 1d, 2d or 3d. Of course, the higher the amount to be won, the smaller the space. To win half a crown (two shillings and sixpence) for instance, the square was blacked in round the edge, leaving a round space about the size of the coin itself. To our utter disbelief, her solitary coin landed right in the middle of the half-crown circle, much to the consternation of the stall-holder who produced a mirror to view it from all angles, but finally had to admit defeat. It is to his credit that he paid out, although there was little that two children could have done about it, in any case. We came away as though we had won the Pools!'

Gala Day was another of the year's highlights, when a long procession would be watched by large crowds lining the route, at least five or six deep, or so it seemed to a small child struggling to get to the front. After all these years, one can still remember the excitement as a distant tinkling was heard, heralding the approach of the bell-man, ringing a hand-bell and leading the procession. (For years the man who performed this duty was the proprietor of a small shop in Newmarket Street). Mrs Gladys Yeadon, too, has happy memories of Gala Day. She writes, 'The Gala was in aid of the Cottage Hospital in Granville Street, (later Skipton R.D.C. Offices and later still pulled down), and from the mid-twenties Whinfield (now Skipton General Hospital). The town dignatories rode in style in limousines. Scouts, Cubs, Guides and Brownies paraded, and there were many classes of Fancy Dress and decorated floats. Collections were made all the way along the route in open flat carts with Scouts and Cubs 'fielding' the coins that missed their targets. For some years the Gala Field was one which was entered at the top of the Bailey. A bridge crossed the tram-way (now filled in) from the 'Rock', and this same

Hospital Gala Float.

bridge gave access on the left to Skipton Woods. The fire-work set-pieces were put up against the back-ground of the Wood, and the dark mass of trees enhanced the display. For me, this was always the best part of the Gala.'

The late Mr Dick Atkinson, born 1880, found that his early memories of the Gala sustained him during later years when he lost his sight. In his mind's eye he recalled how he and his work-mates entered horse-drawn tableaux over a long period. Once, a cart was realistically rigged up as a boat, festooned in fish, and men attired in heavy oilskins carried on an impromptu comedy show, under the heading 'Fishermen of the Mighty Deep', as the cart went through the town. Unfortunately, the fish were by no means as fresh as they might have been, and attracted so many cats that the well-intentioned tableau looked like upsetting the whole procession, and the party was asked to withdraw!

Then there was Moor View Baths and Pleasure Grounds, first erected in 1833 by Dr Dodgson M.D. adapting the old reservoir for this purpose. (The manager's house is now an R.A.F. Club and a housing development covers the site). At one time there were swings, see-saws, a horizontal bar, rings and band stand, and the prestigious Annual Swimming Gala later became an important event. The baths, at the foot of Rombald's Moor, some 435 feet above sea-level, were 75 feet long and 18 feet wide, with six slipper baths, sponge and shower baths and spitoons around the edge! In its early days, it was said that, 'Here young people may enjoy themselves to their heart's content for the modest sum of one penny each.' Learners in the Thirties entered the water at the 3 foot end of the pool, with Mr Jeffrey the manager, holding a long pole in front of them as they took their first tentative strokes. He then pulled the pole away as the learners gained confidence (and depth) leaving them in a 'sink or swim' situation.

We children would mount a few steps at the end of the indoor bath to pop out through a little door which led to the 'Open Air Bath'—in other words, a deep reservoir-like pool. We would then swim diagonally to the western bank, feeling that now we had graduated to the great outdoors, we had well and truly 'arrived'. I understand that the outdoor bath was about 20 feet deep, and as far as I remember there was no supervision outside, but I do not recall any incidents there.

Winter had its own compensations. Mrs Gladys Yeadon recalled very severe winters around 1925-6 when the Springs Canal which leads to the Woods was frozen over, as was the Round Dam in the woods. Tom remembers that Ermysted's Grammar School boarders were allowed to go skating along the dam and on the outside Moorview Bath. Gladys goes on, 'I remember large numbers of people walking on the ice (for the novelty I suppose), and a motor bike being ridden on it. I recall being taken by my parents to the

Hospital Gala Float 1911.

Outdoor Baths, Moorview.

Round Dam one evening. Lanterns were set round the margin, and there were many skaters, some quite expert, doing Figure Eights and waltzing in pairs. A neighbour of ours, whom I thought of as 'old' (probably in her 40s!) delighted me by allowing me to hang on to the back of her skirt, and thus towing me around.'

New Year's Day was a time when one of Skipton's old customs was enacted, and the children of the town 'scrambled' outside the small shops and businesses, (grocers' shops being a particular focus of attention). Driven by the herd instinct, crowds of children would assemble outside a targeted shop, until the groundswell of booing or cheering achieved the desired result. Showers of sweets or coins would be thrown into the road, and a mad scramble ensued. Sometimes, for added excitement, shopkeepers would throw out pre-heated red-hot pennies, but towards the end 'scrambling' became somewhat 'tame', as children queued up for a bright new penny each, and in time the custom came to an end.

Mr Norman Dexter recalls that Skipton was rich in musical ability from the Thirties onwards. Mr Townsend, headmaster of Brougham Street School was a fine musician who was in charge of Cecilia Ladies' Choir and who took pupils to Ilkley Musical Festival. Skipton too, had its own Musical Festival, as it has today. There was a May Day Festival in the Town Hall, with Brougham Street School contributing country dancing and choral singing. The churches also played their part, having capable conductors in Ben Walls and Earl Walls who were associated with Gargrave Road Methodist Church. The Gargrave Road Methodists always rendered the 'Messiah' with top class soloists of national, even international repute. Names included Isobel Bailey (soprano)—'Nobody could sing 'I know that my Redeemer liveth' like Isobel Bailey.' Henry Gill (base) and Peter Dawson (baritone). Clarice Bickerton was a fine local singer. David Jolly was another who enhanced Skipton's musical reputation, also Mr Churcher, conductor at the 'Tin Tabernacle' down Broughton Road, while Hume Wrathall and Mr Wilkinson conducted the Male Voice Choir which took part in many competitions. Nicholas Smith was in charge of the Skipton Permanent Orchestra which gave two concerts a year in either the Plaza or Odeon cinemas, and the Mission Band's concerts were well attended, usually on Sunday evenings.

For those not particularly musically inclined, there was always the 'Pictures' or the 'Flicks', which were then in their hey-day. The three picture houses were well patronised; the Premier, erected as a cinema where Sunwin House now is, the Regal, (later the Odeon and initially the Morriseum) on Keighley Road, and the Plaza (Gem) on Sackville Street. At first silent pictures were screened, with a mere caption to describe the action, but in the early 1920s came the innovation of the 'Talkies'. 'Everybody' went to the Pictures

The Round Dam, Skipton Woods.

on Saturday nights, with people in long queues stretching along the pavement who themselves were occasionally entertained by musicians or even preached at by evangelists.

Couples, and those on their first date, always gravitated to the Pictures, and if found to have been seated on the back row, were subject to knowing winks and nods as here amorous activities could be pursued unseen by anyone behind. At one time an orchestra played at the Odeon, and later appropriate music was provided in the intervals by an organ—so much a part of the atmosphere of the cinema, when usherettes steered patrons towards their seats with flashlights, or glided up and down the carpeted aisles with ice cream.

Many of the films were made in Hollywood. Glamorous actresses emerged from fire and flood without a hair out of place, and films usually ended on a romantic note, fading into the sun-set. Tear-jerking sagas were numerous, and if you emerged into the daylight fighting back the tears, you knew that you had had your money's worth. Morale-boosting epics were popular during the War, and the Gaumont-British News never failed to announce in sonorous tones, 'This is the News, presenting the truth to the free peoples of the world.'

When the annual holiday came round, few people had the money or 'know how' to travel abroad. The mills would 'play' for the week, and a few much-looked-foward-to days in Morecambe or Blackpool was the norm, chugging out of Skipton on the old steam train, and taking pot-luck with the weather, but just as enjoyable for all that.

The days of steam.

XVII
Not cast in the common mould

SKIPTON'S most remembered and best-loved 'characters' are by no means always the rich and famous.

At the east end of the Christ Church burial ground is an interesting tombstone which reads:—

'In memory of Edwin Calvert, son of Richard Calvert, known by the title of The Commander-in-chief. He was the smallest and most perfect man in the world, being under 36 inches in height and weighing 25½ lbs. He died much lamented and deeply regretted by all who knew him, August 7th 1859, aged 17 years.'

No one now remembers Edwin Clavert, but this inscription brought to mind another young man, about a hundred years later—Keith Horner. Keith was also small in stature, but big in cheerfulness, and is similarly remembered with affection by many Skiptonians.

As one privileged to travel with Keith during the 1940s, it is true to say that one always felt the better for having been in his company. 'Little Keith' was very popular, and a born entertainer. At local dances he could sometimes be persuaded to 'do a turn', his favourite ditty being, 'You get no bread with one meat ball,' accompanied by his tap-dancing skills.

It is said that on one occasion Keith came face to face with another gentleman of short stature, who was connected with a visiting circus. To his surprise, the stranger greeted him with, "Hello, Keith!"

"How did you know my name?" asked Keith, in amazement.

"Well," said the other, "As I walked through the town, so many people clapped me on the shoulder and said, 'Hello Keith,' that I realised that I was being mistaken for someone else like myself."

Mr William (Billy) Gelling was a familiar figure in the town during the first half of the century, where he could often be seen, bare-chested, pushing a wooden box with iron wheels. Billy, who lived on Waller Hill, was widely popular and had a great sense of humour. Formerly a rag-gatherer, he accumulated quite a stock of old top-hats, of which he was very proud, often wearing one himself, although he never wore a shirt or overcoat for work. He regularly attended Christ Church, when he would often wear a 'front,' collar and tie, (but no shirt underneath), tail-coat and top hat.

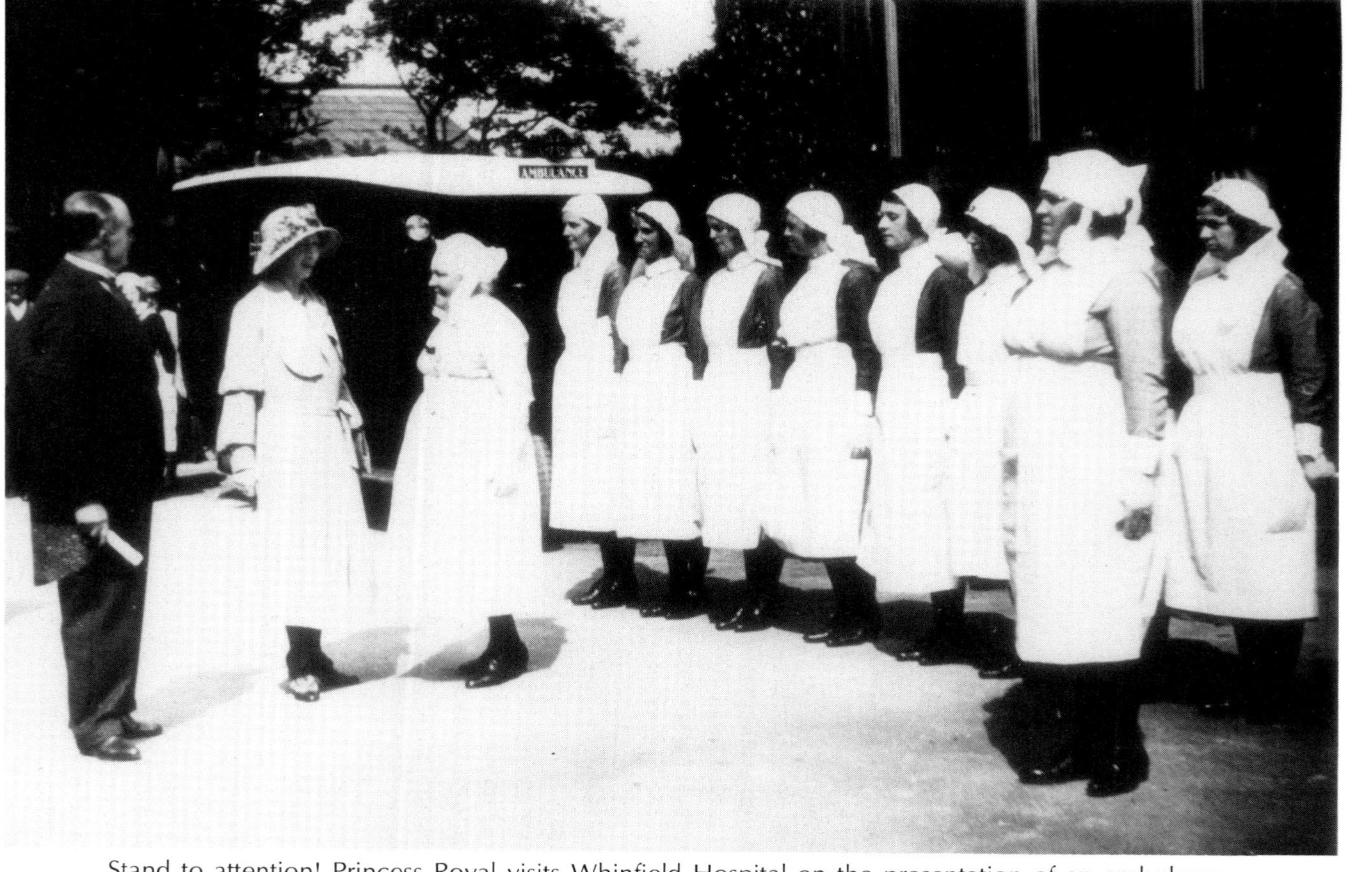

Stand to attention! Princess Royal visits Whinfield Hospital on the presentation of an ambulance.

Billy had the 'official rights' for salvaging coal from the canal near Belle Vue Mills, with his truck and long handled scoop. It is said that as an extra bonus, the boatmen who delivered coal to the mills in canal barges, would sometimes arrange to 'spill' a bit of coal into the water, at the same time putting a mark on the wall so that its position could be located. As a sideline, Billy used to go round the cobblers' shops for discarded clog irons, which he then took to Myers' Rag Shop to be weighed.

Another local character. Henry Ralph, was a familiar figure at Hospital Galas, and is remembered for his rendering of 'The man who broke the bank at Monte Carlo'. Cleave Hargreaves, yet another character, was a little man with a deep voice, who sold newspapers for many years at Ship Corner. Frank Whalley, coal merchant, is remembered for his wit and astuteness. It happened that Skipton Rugby Club had its H.Q. at the Devonshire Hotel, where Frank liked to take a drink. He was sure to have a crowd round him, and sometimes, for fun, he would say, "I've just time for another before bustime," knowing that somebody would get him a drink for the sake of his company. In fact, he only lived just across the road! (Frank himself was a popular and generous man). He always had a horse trimmed up for the Gala, and was distinguishable by his khaki boccy.

A great character and local employer, was Mr Tom Lumb, and the tales about what Tom Lumb said and what Tom Lumb did, are legion. Mr Lumb owned the paper mill, (recently renovated) situated near the canal below Belmont Bridge. He was a blunt man, who called a spade a spade, but his bark was worse than his bite, and many people worked for him loyally, for many years. However, he did not like time-wasting, and the favourite 'tale' at one time doing the rounds, concerned a butcher's shop, which he also owned. The butcher who worked for Tom, happened to have in his shop a butcher's lad from elsewhere, who had called to return some meat. Mr Lumb called in the shop, and seeing the lad gossiping, he asked him what he thought he was doing, and how much a week he earned. The boy told him, whereupon Mr Lumb promptly paid him off—which was fine, except that the lad worked for another butcher!

On another occasion, some building work was being done for Mr Lumb. The joiners were busy sorting planks when Mr Lumb himself appeared, and kept reiterating, (with regard to the planks), "I want the long ones here and the short ones there." Long after the men had got the message he continued to issue the instruction, until finally he took his leave. No sooner had he gone, than one of the joiners said menacingly, "I know what Tom Lumb wants!", and no doubt had something not very palatable in mind. Mr Lumb had not quite been out of earshot, however, He heard the comment, swung round, confronted the man, and asked, "Well, so what DOES Tom Lumb want?" . . .

and the joiner replied innocently, ''Why, he wants the long ones here, and the short ones there, of course!''

Yet Tom Lumb's heart was in the right place. Mr Jim Brayshay recalls how once when the car was broken down and ditched, a passer-by stopped to give help and a welcome shove. He turned out to be Mr Lumb, who after rendering assistance, left them with the words of wisdom, ''A little help is worth a lot of sympathy.''

Mr Lumb was good for Skipton. His one-time home was Whinfield, which he transfered to the town for use as a hospital, and he was a generous benefactor to the Gargrave Road Methodist Church. In an era when we are increasingly influenced by the media, we still need these 'eccentrics' to keep the flame of individuality alive.

XVIII
World War II 1939-1945

THE SECOND World War heralded its coming loud and long. The rise of Hitler meant that there was international crisis after international crisis, when we were continually hauled back from the brink as Hitler gobbled up one country after another, so that when war did break out on September 3rd 1939, it was almost a relief. Even then, the expected bombardments did not come, and there was a 'phoney war' for nearly a year before things really began to 'hot up'. The Skipton district played its part, along with the rest of the nation, as rationing was introduced, sign posts removed, houses requisitioned for war use, and evacuees made their appearance. More and more men and women were called up in the relevant age groups, and the streets gradually filled up with uniforms. For a time, gas-masks were carried about everywhere, but as danger from gas receded, they were abandoned.

On the home front, householders were required to register with one particular grocer for rationed goods, but from time to time extra supplies would come in, when grocers, often unfairly, were accused of putting goods 'under the counter' for more favoured customers. "There won't always be a war on," was a phrase commonly used, indicating that when free to do so, customers would shop elsewhere, (little knowing that all too soon family grocers would be ousted by the supermarkets). Shop windows were full of nothing but cardboard boxes, and if you saw a queue you joined it, not knowing what was at the other end. (The writer remembers once joining a long queue from Woolworth's stretching right round Ship Corner—at the end, a small saucepan.) Human nature being what it is, the Black Market flourished, and 'spivs' were those who managed to make a bit on the side by somehow procuring goods that were in short supply.

As time went on, the district took on a more war-time appearance. 'Pill-boxes' (machine-gun posts) sprouted here and there at strategic points, and the tops of some of the mills were camouflaged in green and brown stripes to break up the outline. When darkness came, the black-out descended, and all windows were covered with shutters or thick black material. The roads were almost deserted, apart from military vehicles in convoy, and what few cars there were, had masks on the headlights, with light filtering through tiny slits. All house-building was suspended, and general maintenance and coats of paint became things of the past.

‘Look-out’ for fire-watchers on Parish Church tower, Second War, complete with castellation!

The Food Office was an essential ingredient of war-time life. Mr Skinner was in charge on its first day of opening on Otley Street, assisted by Miss Joan Thompson (Mrs N. Vaulkhard). Later officials included Miss Pye and Miss Kathleen Riley from Crosshills. Issuing ration books was the first priority, which meant working Saturdays and Sundays with no thought of overtime pay as the work was there to be done, and you had to get on with it. Britishers remained remarkably healthy on a restricted and uninspiring diet, and our survival during those difficult years depended to a large extent on those unsung heroes of the Merchant Navy.

Freedom went out of the window during wartime, when we lived under a virtual dictatorship, and could be directed to any job likely to enhance the war effort, as well as being called upon to fire-watch all night in places of employment or derelict buildings. Any protestors had to face a daunting and unsympathetic Tribunal.

So it was, that in accordance with war-time practice, after a period at the Food Office, Joan was transferred to 'munitions' at the AVRO factory at Yeadon, which necessitated leaving Skipton to live in a hostel at Horsforth. The AVRO factory—then the biggest aircraft factory in Europe under one roof, stood on the site of the present Yeadon Airport Industrial Estate, and was fully camouflaged with imitation trees, hedges, animals and even a duck pond. Here, some 12,000 people were employed, more than 50 per cent women, working a 67-hour, seven-day week. In six years it produced more than 5,000 aircraft, including almost 700 Lancaster Bombers—the planes with which the Vaulkhard family became only too familiar.

Joan has vivid memories of her work dismantling crashed Lancasters. The best part was removing the instrument panels, but most uncomfortable was the 'Dope Shop', where painted bodywork was immersed in solvent, after which the paint had to be scraped off the panels. The effect of the fumes was to make the girls sleepy, but they thought it was going a bit too far when the supervisor came around rapping knuckles to keep them awake!

Many Royal Artillery Soldiers were trained in Skipton, guns being positioned down Engine Shed Lane, and tanks were garaged at the top of Clitheroe Street and Sawley Street. Barbara Mason recalls how they used to churn up the stone kerb edges during their sorties.

Skipton was never a target for the enemy, but night after night, Skiptonians would hear the German planes brrm...brrmming overhead with their own distinctive sound, on their way to Liverpool and Merseyside. Any bombs dropped in this area were odd ones, to release the load perhaps. On Elslack Moor, a stone initialed J.J.D. (J.J. Duckworth) reads:—

'The Great War 1929-1945
Six bombs dropped on this Moor
Sept 16th 1940'

Incendiaries were dropped on Cononley Ings at the same time, and the occasional German plane was spotted in daylight going up the valley, supposedly following the railway line. It was said that a bomb was dropped at Selside which demolished a farm house, killing the unfortunate occupants, who were simply unlucky, surrounded as they were by so much open country. There was strict news censorship throughout the war, and these events were not allowed to be reported in the 'Craven Herald', so that one only learned what was going on by hearsay. There was no mention, for instance of a military aircraft which crashed at Bradley when a wing fell off, killing all six members of the crew. As a nation, we were constantly reminded that 'Careless talk costs lives' and could even be arrested for spreading alarm and despondancy.

The war took a large slice out of young lives, at best disrupting careers and family life, at worst causing marital problems, with women struggling to work and bring up families alone. In time, the dreaded casualties began to come in, some having made the supreme sacrifice, other languishing in Prisoner of War camps ('Stalag' became a very familiar word.) As during the First War, there was an influx of foreign P.O.W.s who in the Second War were accommodated at a camp where the Overdale Caravan Park now is. Both Italian and German prisoners worked on local farms, Some even married local girls and settled down in this country after the war.

A story is told of a couple of young men who decided to spend a holiday in Austria, some time after the war had finished. They were staying at a family-run inn, and one of the youths decided to have a bit of fun at the inn-keepers expense by addressing him in Yorkshire dialect.

Said the youth, "Es ta owt to eyt in t'oil?"

The inn-keeper replied, "Aye, for sewer I ev! What willta 'ev?"

It turned out that he had been a prisoner of war on a farm in Yorkshire, and although he couldn't speak English, he could converse in dialect!

Mr Percy Ogden was headmaster of Ings School during those traumatic years 1941-1945. He was Home Guard warden, in charge from Christ Church to the bottom of Broughton Road. There was then a large and important goods and shunting yard at the railway, (which kept Broughton Roaders awake all night). When the siren went, special attention had to be paid to the Goods Yard. Mr Ogden also looked after stirrup-pumps, (for putting out incendiaries), and gas-masks, and he was on the War Agricultural Committee, (the 'War Ag') looking after allotments and seeing that plenty of lime and seeds were available—usually from Laycock's, who stored lime which was sold at a shilling a bag. Percy started a 'Dig for Victory' campaign, running classes on Saturday mornings, when specialists from Wakefield would demonstrate how to get maximum production from an allotment, using the school strip as an example. He also started the Skipton Young Farmers' Club, as farmers and home-grown food suddenly became of vital importance.

So many local men and women rendered invaluable service in the war effort and in the Services, that it is possible to mention only a few, but their experiences could be duplicated in almost every family.

Typical of the many whose working life was disrupted, is Mr Fred Atkinson, who was called up in 1940 and spent 5 years 8 months in the Black Watch, seeing service in North Africa, Sicily, France, Belgium, Holland and Germany. Meanwhile, at home, his wife, Doreen, drove a motor wagon for the railway, delivering items from the Goods Shed.

Everyone who served in the war had a story to tell. Take, as an example, the experiences of the late Mr Harry Easterby, formerly of Skipton. Harry 'went across' on D-Day, and although he survived the action it was a fortnight before his wife had news of him, and in the meantime she heard of a contemporary of his who had been killed. Understandably, she had to brace herself before daring to pick up the post. Another soldier, veteran of the D-Day landing, described how, amid all the mayhem as the British were coming ashore, a French farmer in a nearby field calmly contunued ploughing, as though nothing was happening! (Or was this man a 'front'?)

Harry Easterby remembered entering Caen, the scene of heavy fighting, where things had not gone according to plan. By this time the Germans had moved on, but the British were still being sniped at and killed, by a hidden sniper who turned out to be a priest-collaborator firing from the church tower.

After the Germans had moved on in one area Jim Brayshay found a cellar full of abandoned maps, showing in detail every part of Britain—all ready for the projected invasion of this country. Among them was a map of our part of Northern England which is now one of Jim's valued possessions.

The experiences of the Vaulkhard brothers of Skipton typify the sacrifices made and the privations endured by that generation which happened to be the right age to be caught up in Hitler's war. The late Mr Norman and Mr James Jardine Vaulkhard were both navigators, trained in Canada, flying in the notorious Lancaster Bombers, many of which, being relatively easy targets, failed to return to base. During the war, a Spitfire pilot once said to the writer, "Give me a Spitfire Fighter anytime for safety, because you are on your own, making your own decisions, whereas in a Lancaster you are one of the crew of six, depending on someone else, in a plane which is not easily manoeverable."

Sadly, James (Jimmy) Vaulkhard was shot down over the Normandy coast, and all six members of the crew perished. According to an eye-witness account, the local inhabitants rushed to the scene and dragged five of the bodies clear of the plane, but before they had time to retrieve the sixth, the

Avro Lancaster Bomber

Germans arrived, and tossed the last body into the sea. Only one had any means of identification, hence although five of the crew are buried together in Normandy, no one is sure which crew member is not amongst them.

Norman Vaulkhard was more fortunate, although he too, was shot down, (near Antwerp), but miraculously landed in a tree without serious injury. He sought help from nearby cottages, but without success as the locals were too afraid to render assistance. While wandering around in his flying gear, he was inevitably spotted by the Germans, who removed him from the scene in a motor-bike and side-car. Eventually, he was transported to Lithuania, where he spent two years as Prisoner of War at Stalag Luft VI, in the company of nearly 300 other Yorkshire airmen. He had no complaints about his treatment, apart from boredom, and spent a lot of time playing bridge. Those below the rank of sergeant had to go out of the camp to work, but this at least kept their minds occupied.

While in Stalag Luft VI, some of the prisoners formed themselves into the White Rose Club, and in May 1944, produced a unique issue of the 'Yorkshire Post'—The 'Kriegie' edition. (An abbreviation of Kriegesfangen for P.O.W.) This magazine was smuggled to England via Sweden, and copies were printed to distribute to next of kin. Mrs Joan Vaulkhard received her copy almost a year later.

Here is a short extract from a poem written for the Kriegie edition by an inmate of the camp, Duggie Sykes, giving an insight into the feelings of the prisoners at the time. Remember, that when this was written the prisoners had no idea how long their incarceration would last, nor could they know with certainty that they would ever see Britain again.

'Homeland. How fortunate once more
You were in times of war,
Breeding those lads so true,
Who fought through toil
And strife and tears,
So you could live anew!'

Perhaps we should reflect on these words. There are some who say that this was all a long time ago, and that it is time the war was forgotten. But while wishing to preserve the peace, we must also keep faith with those who suffered and died, being thankful for the happier circumstances which all now enjoy, and acknowledging that the sacrifices of 'yesterday' made possible the freedom which is ours today.

XIX

Dialect Words (mostly) once in common usage around Skipton

HERE is a list of dialect words and expressions frequently used in and around Skipton between the wars. (If not in the best circles!)

ammost - almost
addle - earn
allus - always
'appen - maybe
asta? - have you?
'awf-baked - a bit simple
ax - ask
aye - yes
back-end - autumn
back-word - cancellation
bahn - going
band - string
bearce, beeasts - cattle
black-clock - black-beetle
bob - shilling
boiling lump - unattractive female
boose - cow standing
boskin - partition between cows
bottom - valley
brass - money
brassen - brazen
bray - hit hard
breaking up - schools going on holiday
breead - bread
breet - bright
brocken - broken
brocken-winded - puffed
caffle - hesitate
canned up - drunk
can't bide it - can't stand it
capped - surprised
clammed - hungry
coil 'oi - coal house
coit - coat
cop 'od of - catch
creeter - creature
croute - grumble
dee - die
don and doff - put on and take off
doing-weel coit - man's long cotton coat
done wi't job! - flabbergasted
don't let on - keep quiet
eeard - heard
eyt - eat
fair to middling - quite good
feight - fight
fest out - cattle on another's land
fettle - condition
flit - move house
fon - found
fotch - fetch
fother - feed cattle
frae - from
frame - apply yourself

fratch - quarrel
friggin about - struggling
fullock - with a spurt
further fetch - ulterior motive
gaiting up - getting loom ready
gallowah - light horse
galluses - braces
ganzie - cardigan
gap 'oil - gateway
gaumless - dense
gawp - stare
gert - big
get agate - start something
getten - got
gill - half a pint
gimmer - female sheep
giste - other people's stock
going down t'nick - going
worst way
haw aye - oh yes
hawf - half
heald - warp threads go
through eyes of healds
hey lands, hey! - the ultimate
hig - fit of temper
hissel - himself
hoined - strained, nattered
hoist - a lift
house - living room
if owt 'appens 'im - if he dies
ivver - ever
jock - food
jolloped - the 'trots'
kall - gossip
kalling 'oil - meeting place
ket - rubbish
kisty - pernickety about food
kit - large milk container
kitle - man's blue cotton jacket
kittle - on edge, tricky
laiking - playing
laithe - barn
'let on' someone - come
across, meet
leet - light
lig - lie
lish - nimble
living tally - unmarried
loin - lane
loosing - coming out of mills or
school
lugs - ears
marra to - matching
marred - spoilt (child)
marlocking about - messing about
mash - brew tea
mawked - grub infested (sheep)
mawngy - bad tempered
meeadless - ineffectual
melder - in a muddle
middling of - a lot of
muild - muddle
mullock - mess
mun - must
naguing away - parsistent ache
nay - no
noan - none
noan so bad - feeling fine
nobbut - only
nobbut middling - not so good
off cumd'n - someone from away
'oil - hole, place, anywhere
oppen - open
out of fettle - poorly
Ow do? - How are you?
Owt fresh? - Any news?
partly what - not completely
pawping about - getting nowhere
peeak - peak, perch
peyling about - rushing about
picked calf - aborted calf
pined - hungry

piseball - ball game using hands not bat
plague - tease
pobs - bread and milk
pow - haircut
preycher - preacher
privy - closet, loo
provven - provender
pund - pound
quid - a pound (money)
rare do - an event that went well
ratty - bad tempered
reight - right
reycher in - textile worker
rive - tear down
room (the) - the parlour
roaky - wet, slushy
rowt iron - wrought iron
sam 'od of - get hold of
scratting about - messing about
set someone back - walk part way home with
Set your stall out - apply yourself
Sha, shoo - she
shippon - cattle shed
shop - any sort of place
shape thissel! - apply yourself!
sidle up to - creep up to
singlet - vest
sithee! - look!
slack set up - not feeling like doing much
slopstone - stone sink
spayned - lambs taken from mother
stalled - fed up
starved - hungry
summat and nowt - of no account
sump 'oil - wet place in field
swaled - melting (of candles)
swathe - row of new-mown hay
tackler - overlooker
tak - take
tanner - sixpence
tup - ram
ten bob - ten shillings
tent - mind looms for
termorn t'neet - tomorrow night
tew - work hard
tha, thee, thou, ta - you
think on - be sure to remember
thoile - bring yourself to do something
threeap - argue repeatedly
threp, threp me down - continued arguing
throng - busy
threepenny dodger - silver 3d bit
trashy weather - wet and puddly
temmed - poured
wacken - waken
wake - weak
wark - work
watter - water
weel - well
well, woll - while, until
westcoit - waistcoat
wether - castrated lamb
wheer? - where?
wick-thing - creepy crawler
wi' - with
wilta? - will you?
wishin - cushion
wovven up - finished
wycherd - wet shod
wye - female calf
yow - ewe, female sheep

A lot of dialect was spoken before the Second War, particularly in the Craven villages. Now, fifty years on, it is rapidly dying out. Commonly understood in Craven, it was unintelligible to people who were not Northerners.

The following 'tale' illustrates the point:—

During the War a U.S. airman supposedly baled out of an aeroplane and landed by parachute on the outskirts of Skipton, although he had no idea where he was.

Hearing two women approaching, he hid himself behind the hedge, while he listened to their conversation to see if he could get his bearings.

The conversation went like this:—

'Oo washe wi'?'
'She war wi' Willee?'
'Washee?'

— And the airman shot himself because he thought he had landed in China!

Here are some Northern expressions, once commonly used.

Drop off t'perch - die
A wink's as good as a nod to a blind 'os. (blind horse)
Put t'wood in t'thoile - shut the door
As throng as Throp's wife - very busy
Messing in t'toits - messing about
Lost wi' yersel - fed up, don't know what to do next
It's a beggar - It's a bad job!
Keep t'band in t'nick - try to agree
Get out o't'gate - shift!
Side the table - clear the table
Like greeased leetning - fast
Winter has picked its cawf - early snow
Wheer's ta bahn? - where are you going?
Fist full o'brass - lots of money
... as though dead lice are dropping off you! - need to get a move on
The little white hen that never laid away - a goody goody
Allus in t'field when you should be in t'loin (lane) - never getting it right
Strong in t'tharm and wake in t'heead - a bit simple
Fair done wi't'job - taken aback
All man, shirt and pocket 'oil - all show and no substance

Of course, dialect was superior to, and different from, sloppy speech. But since so many people talk 'cut glass' these days, see if you can own up to recognising the meaning of the following, also commonly used expressions.

Thallattergerranutha
Oowasheewee?
Supweeim?
It dunt marrer
Owduzeeno?
Thallattadubaht
Abberritint
Astasinowtonim?
Gerronweeit
Estaitwithee
Abberitwornt
Sup?
Tintintin
Gerrodont
Itwornowtutsort
Estafonit?

Bibliography

Skipton Parish Church Registers
The Book of Skipton by Geoffrey Rowley
Old Skipton by Geoffrey Rowley
The History of Skipton Parish Church by Joe Wiseman
Sale Catalogue Skipton Castle Estate 1956
Guide to Skipton and District c 1907
A Sense of the Past by Graham Nown
Year Books of Skipton Urban District Council
Friends of Giggleswick Parish Records
Rekindling the Sparks of Spencer by H. Woledge
Through the Eye of a Needle by H.E. Blythe
The Charmed Land of Craven by Edmund Bogg
The Tempests of Broughton by M.E. Lancaster
Whitaker's History of Craven
West Riding Schools' Bulletin
Craven Household Almanac 1901